FIRST STEPS IN

FIRST STEPS IN WINEMAKING

A complete month-by-month guide to winemaking (including the production of cider, perry and mead) in your own home, with over 130 tried and tested recipes.

6th EDITION

13th Impression - February 1980

By
C. J. J. BERRY
(*Editor, The Amateur Winemaker*)

Amateur Winemaker Publications Ltd., Andover, Hants

Printed in Great Britain by:
· Standard Press (Andover) Ltd., South Street, Andover, Hants.

SBN 0 900841 40 0

Cover by Angel Studios
Photographs by C. Green and J. Griffin
Line illustrations by Rex Royle

About this book

THIS little book really started as a collection of recipes, reliable recipes which had appeared in the monthly magazine, "The Amateur Winemaker". First published in January 1960, it was an instant and phenomenal success, for over 1¼ million copies have been sold, and it is now recognised as the best "rapid course" in winemaking available to the beginner.

As new developments occurred in winemaking and fresh knowledge became available so "First Steps" has been continually amended and up-dated, and for this sixth edition it has been again revised to bring it into line with modern practice, and fresh illustrations included. Metric and U.S. measures are given as well as British ones.

Those who are in need of recipes, and who have probably just fallen under the spell of this fascinating hobby of ours, will also want to know more of its technicalities, so this book includes a wealth of practical tips and certain factual information that any winemaker would find useful. In particular, the hydrometer, ignored in many books on winemaking, has been dealt with simply but adequately . . . you will find this small book a mine of useful information.

The original recipes are there, over 130 of them, with quite a few others, and they are all arranged in the months of their making, so that you can pursue your winemaking all the year round with this veritable Winemakers' Almanac. And as your winemaking experience grows there is no doubt that you will wish to extend your experiments to making wines like those of commerce, making your own liqueurs, growing your own vines, brewing beer, making mead, or cooking with your own wines. All of these activities, and more, are catered for in the "Amateur Winemaker" library of specialised paperbacks, detailed at the end of this book. There are over 40 titles to choose from, and you will find them fascinating reading.

But for the present, get started with "First Steps in Winemaking". I hope you will enjoy this book as much as I have enjoyed writing it . . . best wishes for successful winemaking!

C. J. J. BERRY.

A fascinating craft

IF you are toying with the idea of trying your hand at winemaking, delay no longer. Go right ahead! By doing so you will be joining the thousands of happy folk who, in recent years, have discovered this intriguing and rewarding hobby. It is, indeed, a pastime which truly "brings its own rewards", for there can be few pleasures to equal that of being able to offer a friend, and enjoy with him, a glass of one's own wine.

In the last 20 years there has been an astonishing growth of home winemaking in Britain; wine, it is true, has been made here for centuries, but sugar scarcity during World War II and lack of opportunity debarred many from taking up the pastime, and it was left to the few to keep our craft alive. Now, however, it is attracting the interest of thousands, and scientific developments and the spread of winemaking knowledge have made it possible for anyone to produce a palatable wine in their own home.

In this country there is absolutely no restriction upon how much wine you make as long as it is entirely for your own consumption, but since no duty has been paid upon it *not a drop must be sold*, or you will be in trouble with the law. This prohibition, it should be noted, may well be held to extend to "cheese and wine" parties using home-made wine if a charge is made for admission, and to the raffling of home-made wines, even for a good cause.

Above all, note that distilling is both dangerous, in that alcohols which are not safely potable may be produced, and illegal, carrying very heavy penalties. The same is true of the separation of alcohol by freezing; the offence is in the separation of alcohol by distillation "or any other means". Do not try either process: the risks, both physical and legal, make them just not worth the candle.

What you will need

DO not, at the outset, buy a lot of expensive equipment: it is better to *start* making wine with what you have—you probably have in your kitchen already some of the essentials—

4

and then to acquire the rest by stages as the necessity arises. For a start you will undoubtedly need some kind of boiler, and if you can lay your hands on one that will hold three to five gallons it will prove ideal. Failing that. you can "make do" with a one-gallon or one-and-a-half gallon saucepan.

Avoid containers and utensils of iron. brass and copper, which may be affected by acids and impart hazes and flavours to your wine; use only boilers of aluminium or sound—unchipped—enamel ware.

You will also need a large vessel in which to do your soaking, or mashing, and one of three to five gallons is ideal. It is preferable to have one in a high-density synthetic material such as polypropylene—the harder and whiter the material the better—but if for reasons of cheapness and availability you decide to use a plastic dustbin—and thousands do—remember that the colourants used in some bins (which were not intended for food use) may well be toxic, and it is therefore advisable to use a "liner" of limp, transparent polythene. But preferably buy a "brewing bin" designed for the purpose from Woolworths or wine shops.

Alternatively you can use an earthenware crock of some sort. Tall, cylindrical ones are the most convenient, since they are easier to cover and take up less floor space than the "bread-pan" variety. They should be hard salt-glazed, since lead glaze can have poisonous results. True it is rarely encountered on domestic vessels nowadays, but one does occasionally come across it on very old ones, or on those of Middle Eastern origin, so this warning needs to be issued! Salt glaze is hard, but lead glaze is soft, and can be dented with the thumbnail. You probably already have a polythene bucket, and will find this extremely useful for small quantities.

Also obtain several one-gallon jars for fermenting—those with "ear" handles are the most popular—and some rubber bungs and corks to fit. These jars are now not always easy to obtain and you may have to make do with poly-propylene or polythene containers, either cubes or bottles. But *try* always to stick to glass; it is always safer and can convey no flavour. On no account omit to buy or make as

for boiling

BOILER BUCKET

SAUCEPAN

FISH KETTLE

USEFUL
FOR   HOME

for mashing —

BREWING BIN

"ALI - BABA"

BUCKET

for straining

SIEVE

MUSLIN

and fermenting

"EX-WINE" FIVE

1 GALLON JAR

EQUIPMENT
WINEMAKING

for clearing

FILTER PAPER

JELLYBAG

BOOTS

VINBRITE

HARRIS

VINAMAT

for storage

CASKS, STONE JARS, GLASS JARS, WINE BOTTLES.

BORER

FLOGGER

CORKING TOOL

CORKS

CAPSULES

LABELS

many fermentation traps (see separate chapter) as you are likely to need, for they are indeed the winemaker's best friend.

You will also find it useful to collect half-gallon bottles (Winchesters) and a supply of white wine bottles—NOT squash or sauce bottles, *please!*— and corks or stoppers to fit. It is false economy to use old corks, which may infect your wine; always use new corks, and soak them in a sterilising solution before insertion. Alternatively. buy some of the new plastic stoppers which can be used over and over again, after sterilising by boiling water.

You will find a funnel. a really large polythene one, most useful, and it is worth obtaining some nylon sieves or material for straining purposes. Do not forget to obtain, too, a supply of Campden tablets (ordinary fruit-preserving tablets) which have many uses in winemaking, and a rubber or polyvinyl tube for siphoning the wine off the yeast deposit. A colander, scales, a wooden or polypropylene spoon, and measuring jugs you will already have in your kitchen.

Refinements

THESE are the bare essentials, but undoubtedly as you progress in winemaking you will add other pieces of desirable equipment—a thermometer, a hydrometer for calculating the strength of your wine, glass tubing for taking samples, small funnels, casks, stone jars, tie-on labels for jars and stick-on labels for bottles, a corking device, a cork borer, filtering apparatus, a bottle cleaning brush, and perhaps a small press or one of the quite inexpensive juice extractors now obtainable which can do so very much to remove the "cookery" from winemaking and make it that more pleasurable. You may even go to the length of wanting to be *entirely* sure of accuracy, so much so that you will need some acid measuring equipment. But there is no need to bother about all this at the outset. That is the beauty of winemaking, you can tackle it as you please, either in comparatively simple fashion with the help of recipes, or by going the whole hog and delving more fully into its scientific side, making up country wines to suit your taste in the light of your experience.

Wine vocabulary

Aerobic Fermentation: A fermentation conducted in the presence of air. Usually the first part of the fermentation process.

Anaerobic Fermentation: A fermentation from which air is excluded; the second part of the fermentation process.

Body: The fullness of a wine.

Campden Tablets: Useful in winemaking for various sterilisation or purification purposes. They supply sulphur dioxide in convenient form.

Carbon Dioxide: The colourless, odourless gas given off by a fermenting liquor.

Concentrate: The juice of white or red wine grapes concentrated and sold in tins or packs.

Dry: A wine is said to be dry when all the sugar in it has been used up by the fermentation: it is also said to have "fermented right out".

Fermenting (or working): The process brought about by yeast acting upon sugar to produce alcohol and carbon dioxide.

Fermentation Trap (or Air-Lock): A little gadget used to protect the fermentation from infection by the vinegar fly. Also called a "bubbler".

Fining: Removing suspended solids from a cloudy wine by filtering or adding wine finings.

Flogger: A wooden tool for banging corks home.

Fortification: Increasing the strength of wine beyond that possible by natural fermentation by adding spirit.

Hydrometer: An instrument for measuring the weight (or sugar content) of a liquid.

Hydrometer Jar: The jar in which a hydrometer is floated for a reading to be taken.

Filtering Apparatus: For clearing wine thoroughly.

Lees: The deposit of yeast and solids formed during fermentation.

Liquor: The unfermented, sugar-containing liquid which will eventually be wine.

Malo-Lactic Fermentation: See p. 36.

Must: The pulp or combination of basic ingredients from which a wine is made.

Nutrient: Nitrogenous matter added to the liquor to boost the action of the yeast; yeast food.

Proof: Proof spirit contains 57.1% alcohol. 70 deg. proof really means 70% of proof spirit. Thus ordinary proprietary bottles of spirit will contain only 40% alcohol by volume. In the U.S. Proof is 50% alcohol by volume.

Racking: Siphoning the wine off the lees to clear and stabilise it.

Stable: A wine is said to be stable when there is no danger of further fermentation.

Stopper: A cork or polythene bottle closure with a projecting cap.

Straining: Removing the solids from the must.

Vinegar: Wine which has "gone wrong".

(For a more detailed glossary, see *The Winemaker's Dictionary*.)

Cleanliness

COMPLETE cleanliness is most important to the winemaker: all his vessels, bottles and equipment must be not only visually clean but chemically clean. Airborne yeasts and vinegar and other bacteria can only be kept at bay by constant vigilance, and the simplest answer to the problem is to make up a sterilising solution.

Dissolve two Campden tablets (ordinary fruit-preserving tablets, which are sodium metabisulphite and will give you the sulphur dioxide you need) and a saltspoon of citric acid in a pint of water.

Make up a quantity of this: use it to sterilise your bottles and equipment; but note that it must be kept in tightly-corked bottles or it will deteriorate. Use it to rinse all your equipment before and after use and also to sterilise your fermenting vessels. A small quantity can be used to do many jars and bottles by pouring it from one to the other, corking, rolling, and shaking each one in turn so that all parts of the interior are moistened. Wipe round the neck of the bottle with cottonwool dipped in the solution.

This is a much quicker, simpler (and safer) method than using boiling water or "baking in the oven", as some books recommend.

Glass jars, carboys and bottles can safely
kept sterile if half an inch of the solution is left
of each, and they are tightly corked.

If you cannot obtain Campden tablets, ma
a stock solution of potassium (or sodium) m
($K_2S_2O_4$) by crushing 5 oz. of the crystals in warr
making the quantity up to 1 gallon (100 gms. to 3
as follows:

For sterilising corks, barrels, bottles and apparatus:
8 fluid oz. of stock solution, plus $\frac{1}{4}$ oz. citric acid, made
up to 1 gallon with water (250 ml., plus 10 gms. citric
acid, made up to 5 litres);

To purify the "must" before fermentation: $\frac{1}{2}$ fl. oz. of
stock solution per gallon of "must"; (20 ml. to 5 litres).

To sterilise completely a "must" or juice: $1\frac{1}{2}$ fl. oz. per
gallon of "must" (50 ml. to 5 litres).

To prevent fermentation in hot weather double that
quantity might be needed.

If you do not wish to go to the trouble of making up
your own sterilant, use one of the excellent proprietary ones
available, Chempro or Silana pf.

Modern developments in brewery cleaning chemicals
have resulted in the production of multi-action products.
I personally now use one of these—Chempro—because it has
been formulated to clean and sterilise *in one operation*. It
swiftly removes and rinses away any surface dirt and bacteria,
leaving bottles and jars sparkling clean and completely
sterile, with virtually no effort.

What wine is

TRUE wine is the product of the grape, we are often
reminded, but any winemaker of experience will assure you
that we have no cause to feel in any way ashamed of the
"country wines" which can be produced from our native
fruits, berries and flowers. Many of these sound wines, robust
or delicate according to character, dry or sweet according to
one's taste, are truly wines in their own right, quite capable
of standing comparison with many which can be obtained

11

cially. You may find this difficult to believe, but, ... you have produced what you *think* is a good wine, compare it with a commercial wine of similar type, and we guarantee you will be pleasantly surprised.

And once one understands the basic principles it is by no means difficult to make wine at home. True, the more you make, the more discerning and critical your palate will become, and the more you will find yourself seeking to capture in your own wines those elusive qualities which go to make a great wine. Even the complete beginner, it is true, can by following a recipe produce a sound and satisfying wine—often without knowing how or why! It is, however, infinitely better to understand the principles of the craft.

Our country wines, one might say, have four main ingredients initially: (1) Yeast, (2) Sugar, (3) Flavouring and (4) Water. There are others which play their parts, notably acids, tannin and substances which nourish the yeast, but for simplicity's sake we will ignore them for the moment, and deal with them later. Time, the time required for maturation, also plays an important part.

Of these main ingredients undoubtedly the most important is YEAST. Yeast is a minute living organism which brings about fermentation, and if the fermentation is to be successful the yeast must be given ideal conditions in which to work. Those conditions are found in a sugary, slightly acid solution such as fruit juice, when certain other yeast nutrients are present and when the temperature is favourable, say 65 degrees to 75 degrees F. (18–24 degrees C.).

Fermentation

THE alcohol which we seek as an ingredient of our wine is a by-product of the yeast's process of self-reproduction.

When the yeast is put into a sugary solution, it begins to multiply vigorously, and in the complex chemical processes which ensure, the sugar is converted roughly half to alcohol by weight and half to carbon dioxide—the bubbles in your beer, wine, cider or champagne.

It is an encouraging thought that for every bubble you see in your wine there is an equal weight of alcohol! The

12

fermentation will be in two stages, but there is no distinct dividing line. The first, the aerobic ("with air") fermentation, will be comparatively vigorous, perhaps with some froth, but may last only five or six days. The wine will then settle down to the secondary, anaerobic ("without air") ferment, which will be much quieter and which towards the end may be barely discernible. This may last two, three, or four months, or even longer.

Temperature plays an important part. Above 100°F. (38°C.) the yeast will certainly be killed; at too low a temperature it will ferment only very slowly, if at all. A fermentation should be started off at about 70°F. (21°C.), the secondary fermentation should be at about 65°F. (16°C.), and the finished wine should be stored at 50° to 55°F. (10–13°C.). So the temperatures are easy to remember—70°, 60°, 50°F. (or 20°, 15°, 10°C.). A slow quiet fermentation usually produces better wine that a fast, over-vigorous and short one, and there is no need to be fussy within 5°F.

During the secondary fermentation it is wise to employ a device called a fermentation trap, or air lock, which both cuts off the air supply to the yeast and protects your wine from bacterial infection, of which more later.

As the fermentation proceeds, so the alcohol content increases, until finally it reaches a concentration (usually about 16–17% alcohol by volume) which is such as to inhibit the yeast, preventing any further activity. Any sugar still left in the wine then remains only as a sweetening agent. Once the fermentation is finished the wine will not normally become any stronger no matter how long it is kept, although it will undoubtedly mellow with maturity. So discount all the stories you hear on the lines ". . . and this wine was 40 years old; it had become as strong as whisky!"

The vinegar fly

THE worst possible mishap which can befall a winemaker is to have his wine at one stage or another turn to vinegar (from the French *vinaigre:* "sour wine"), which it can quite easily do if vinegar bacteria are allowed access to it. These bacteria are, like yeasts, present everywhere about us, but are sometimes introduced to the wine by infected equipment, or by that obnoxious carrier the vinegar fly (*drosophila melanogaster*). This tiny fly, which appears as if by magic around any fermenting liquor or fruit, is the winemaker's biggest enemy; it must at all costs be kept from your wine. If it gains access to it the liquor, instead of turning to alcohol, may turn to vinegar, and you will have the sad task of pouring it down the drain or using it for cooking, for it will be quite irreclaimable.

The wine can be attacked by bacteria, either airborne or carried by the fly, at any stage, and that is why you *must* cover the first ferment closely with a thick cloth. The principal danger, however, occurs not so much then, when the ferment is vigorous, as during the slow, quiet secondary fermentation.

The fermentation trap

IT is then that one needs to employ a fermentation trap. This is a simple device, being in effect an air-lock, and we illustrate what is undoubtedly the most popular and com-

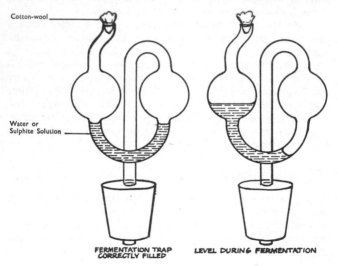

Cotton-wool

Water or
Sulphite Solution

FERMENTATION TRAP
CORRECTLY FILLED

LEVEL DURING FERMENTATION

monly used pattern, a glass U-tube with two bulbs. Similar ones are now made in plastic.

This is inserted in the bung or cork of the fermenting vessels so as to be an airtight fit (this is important, or the lock will not work), and a good tip is to use rubber bungs rather than corks to ensure that there is no leakage. It is advisable to grease the glass trap's stem lightly and hold it in a thick cloth when pushing it home, to avoid the risk of breakage and a hand badly cut by jagged glass. The bottom of the glass stem must be above the level of the fermenting liquor; a half to three-quarters of an inch is normally sufficient, as long as the liquor is not frothing so vigorously as to force it out through the trap.

The U-bend of the trap is then filled with water, to the bottom of the bulbs, and in the water is dissolved one-eighth of a Campden tablet. Thus, even if a vinegar fly gets into the water, and meets an untimely end, your wine will be safe, whereas, if you have plain water in your trap it may become infected with the bacteria from the dead fly. In that case, since the inner end of the water is in aerial contact with your wine, it is still possible for your wine to be infected. So always use this small quantity of sulphite in the bend of your traps, and renew it every month or so. Alternatively, use in the trap glycerine of borax, which is less volatile and will not deteriorate. Yet another method is to use plain water, but to plug the top of the trap with a tiny tuft of cotton wool to deny dust and flies access.

The fermentation trap, incidentally, has a secondary purpose. The yeast, for the reproductive process which it first employs, needs oxygen.

When, by means of the fermentation trap, we cut off its air supply, we force it to turn to a secondary method of self-reproduction which it can use without oxygen, and which is appreciably more productive of alcohol. Of this, naturally, we are wholly in favour!

The air-lock is also a valuable indicator as to when fermentation is finished.

As the wine ferments, it gives off carbon dioxide, which quickly builds up a pressure within the fermentation jar or bottle, and then pushes its way through the solution in the trap with quite a musical "blup . . . blup . . . blup". This, you will find, is quite fascinating to watch. As the ferment proceeds, the bubbles will pass ever more slowly until finally the solution in the trap remains poised and no more gas passes. It is then a good idea to move the jar into a warm room for five or six days to see if any further activity develops. If not, it can be assumed that the fermentation has finished . . . but make sure that your cork or bung is still air-tight and that gas is not escaping through it or from its junction with the tube of the trap, or naturally the trap will not work. Rubber bungs are best; corks need to be waxed.

Making your own

There are several other patterns of air-lock on the market (we illustrate several) and you will eventually decide for yourself which you prefer, and may well even make your own. A plastic or glass tube leading down into an aspirin bottle or yeast phial containing sulphite solution and secured to the fermenting vessel with sticky tape, will answer quite well as long as you remember to remove the phial before uncorking the jar. If you do not, the sulphite solution will be siphoned back into your wine as you withdraw the cork and thus reduce the pressure inside the fermenting bottle. It should be noted that this minor disaster can also happen if the pressure inside the fermenting vessel happens to drop below that of the surrounding atmosphere; the sulphite in the trap will be sucked back into the wine, which is bad for the wine and worse for the temper.

One type of lock which has become increasingly popular in recent years is what might be called the cup type, which is available in several patterns. Many like this type of lock because it is not so fragile as the glass bubbler, but it is not so satisfying to watch or listen to! It consists of a cup into which the tube from the fermentation jar rises, and inverted over the end of the tube is another, smaller-diameter, cup. Sulphite solution is poured into the trap and when gas is given off by the ferment it lifts the inner cup up and down to escape beneath its rim, through the solution. As with the glass bubbler, one needs to inspect the trap from time to

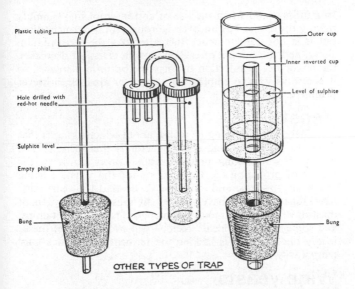

Labels on the diagram:
Plastic tubing
Hole drilled with red-hot needle
Sulphite level
Empty phial
Bung
Outer cup
Inner inverted cup
Level of sulphite
Bung

OTHER TYPES OF TRAP

time to make sure that it still contains plenty of solution, and that too much has not evaporated.

This problem one avoids entirely by using the latest kind of trap, which is really simply a screw cap for a 1-gallon jar embodying a little ball valve, a ball-bearing which is lifted by any gas pressure to allow carbon dioxide to escape, but which drops again and seals the jar when no gas is being given off. Neat and effective, but not very entertaining . . . .

One simple idea is to use an ordinary rubber balloon, stretching it over the neck of the bottle. The pressure of the gas will inflate the balloon, and when inflation ceases the ferment is finished. For wide-necked jars or crocks one can use a sheet of polythene, secured with a stout rubber band. This, too, will be bulged out by the pressure of the gas which will escape from beneath the band.

Some winemakers do not use locks at all, but content themselves with plugging the neck of the fermentation jar with cotton wool. This is an excellent idea for the first few days of fermentation, when the yeast needs plenty of oxygen to multiply, and when the use of cotton wool may simplify tidying up if one has an overvigorous, frothy fermentation, but it is not good practice thereafter. As the fermentation slows, and the amount of carbon dioxide given off decreases, the possibility of infection by airborne bacteria *increases*, so it is always wise to employ some form of air-lock, however primitive.

Yeasts

THE essential thing to realise about winemaking is that the most important and central factor is the YEAST. The whole of winemaking practice really comes down to the matter of providing ideal conditions for the yeast, a living organism, to thrive and multiply. To do that the yeast must have sugar, it must have warmth, it must have oxygen, it must have a certain amount of nitrogenous matter, vitamins, and some acid. The ideal "recipe" will provide all of these; if any one of them is lacking the ferment may "stick", or temporarily stop.

Wine yeasts

ONE of the big strides which has been made in wine-making is that there are now available to the amateur many excellent varieties of special wine yeasts, in either culture or tablet form. Their value is unquestioned, for there are in-numerable varieties of yeasts, all with different characteristics, and just as some are more suitable for baking or beer-brewing, so others are better for the production of quality wine. A good wine yeast has a high alcohol tolerance (i.e., it will allow the wine to ferment further and be that much stronger before it succumbs) it will form a firmer sediment, making racking much simpler, and it will be less prone to impart "off" flavours to the wine.

It is possible to obtain Port, Sherry, Madeira, Tokay, Malaga. Champagne, Sauternes, Pommard, and Burgundy yeasts, to mention only a few.

These yeasts are laboratory-cultured from the yeasts on the grapes in the place of origin, and it is great fun to experiment with them, and see the different nuances of flavour that they confer.

18

But do not imagine that you will obtain, say, a port simply by using a port yeast. The ingredients must be suitable as well. If they are, you are certainly more likely to obtain a port-like wine by using a true port yeast; the flavour will be unimpaired, and you will have the other advantages already mentioned.

It is naturally advisable, when using these specialised yeasts, to employ them in "musts" which will be sympathetic to them, i.e., a Port or Burgundy yeast in a red wine such as elderberry, sloe or damson, and a Champagne yeast in a sparkling wine. The beginner will do best, however, to experiment first with a good general-purpose wine yeast. One can also obtain a fairly good range of yeasts especially suitable for lager, beers and ales.

Many winemakers, one must admit, still adhere to baker's or brewer's yeasts, but it is a pity to do so without having tried some of the excellent true wine yeasts now on the market. They are certainly worth while for one's "special" wines and are by no means as expensive as they at first appear, since they can be propagated and carried on from one wine to another. Wine yeast, granulated yeast, yeast cultures, yeast tablets, baker's yeasts, brewer's yeasts, liquid yeasts ... all will make wine—of varying quality—and which yeast you use is a matter of personal preference.

Making up a starter bottle

NOWADAYS there are so many types of wine yeast readily available, and so much work has been put into their development, that in most cases they can be bought comparatively cheaply in a granular and liquid form which permits of their being added direct to the must. Sometimes, however, a wine yeast will be supplied in only a small quantity and will have to be "activated" for use. All this means is that you start it working, and therefore multiplying, so as to build up a much larger number of active yeast cells for introduction to the "must". The principle is the same in most cases.

Instead of adding the wine yeast direct to the "must", one starts it off in a specially-prepared bottle of sterilised fruit juice of some sort, and nutrient, and then, when the contents of the "starter bottle" are fermenting vigorously, they are added to the "must". The yeast thus has a much better chance of succeeding, since it is already in full activity.

The snag, of course, is that one has to remember to activate the yeast in this way about 48 hours before it is likely to be needed, to allow time for this starter fermentation to get under way. Once a yeast has been activated, this problem diminishes, for a little of it can always be kept back and "grown on" in another starter bottle by adding more fruit juice, water, sugar and nutrient, and the process can be repeated *ad infinitum* as long as care is taken to keep the yeast under sterile conditions.

For the starter juice, one can use either the juice from which the wine is to be made (if some can be obtained beforehand), or some other fruit juice. Since you need half a pint of it the flavour of your wine will not be affected materially if you use a different juice from that of the bulk. To this add an ounce of sugar. Another good starter is a tablespoonful of pure malt extract, a tablespoonful of granulated sugar, the juice of a lemon, and half a pint of water.

Whichever you use, bring it to the boil in an aluminium or sound enamel saucepan to sterilise it, and then allow it to cool before adding your yeast culture.

It is then only necessary to plug the neck of the bottle or container with cotton wool and stand it in a comfortably warm place (70°F, or 21°C) for the yeast to get going. Give the bottle an occasional shake and after a while tiny bubbles will be seen rising to the periphery of the liquid. Note that with wine yeasts there is no showy, frothy fermentation as with baker's yeasts or beer yeasts, and sometimes the fermentation bubbles are barely evident, unless one taps or shakes the bottle. After about two or three days, however, the starter bottle should be in full ferment and the tiny bubbles will clearly be seen rising to the surface. It should then be shaken well to disperse the yeast thoroughly in the liquid, and the starter poured into the bulk of the "must". One such starter bottle should be enough for 5–10 gallons of must.

If you wish to use the starter bottle at intervals over a period make a starter from four ounces of orange and two ounces of lemon juice (preferably strained), plus four ounces of water and one ounce of sugar. When the yeast has been added and it is fermenting three-quarters of it can be used to activate a brew, and the remaining quarter can be topped up with juice made in the same way and will after a week or so also be fermenting and ready to use.

Wine yeast is also sold in tablet and in liquid form, and as a compound, complete with its nutrients (e.g., Formula '67) but all of these are preferably activated in the same way before use, though one can often get a fermentation going by adding them direct to the must. Individual suppliers provide detailed instructions with their yeasts, so there is no need to worry; you will find it quite simple.

Baker's yeast, brewer's yeast, or granulated yeast (the packeted variety) can be added direct to the liquor. Baker's yeast should be fresh. It is best added when the temperature of the liquor is lukewarm, about 70°F. (21°C.). These will give you a more vigorous and frothy ferment than a wine yeast; this does not help the wine, but it perhaps does help someone who is just starting winemaking and who wants to be sure that a ferment really *has* got going.

In all the recipes in this book use a wine yeast where possible, or failing that, 1 level teaspoonful of a good granulated yeast per 1 gallon of liquor.

Beginners often worry about exactly how much yeast to add but as long as one has enough to get the fermentation going reasonably quickly the quantity is not critical, since the first thing the yeast does is to multiply rapidly. Thus, when making, say, five gallons, one does not necessarily need five times as much yeast as for one. Either make up a starter bottle, or, if you are adding the yeast direct to the must, double or treble the quantity.

"No yeast" recipes

INCIDENTALLY, beware of all recipes which omit any mention of yeast; there is no such thing as a "no yeast" recipe for the simple reason that without yeast there can be no fermentation of the sort we want. Yeasts are everywhere about us—in the air, in the soil, the bloom on fruit, in milk,

21

in our mouths—and will find their way into a fermentable liquor. If you use a "no yeast" recipe, you are really simply relying upon any natural yeast which may be on the fruit you used or, if you killed that with boiling water or sulphite, upon any airborne yeast which may find its way into your brew . . . you *may* get a fermentation but the result may be not at all what you hope.

How yeast nutrient helps

TO obtain the best possible fermentation the yeast, like most living organisms, must have both food and oxygen. Like human beings, it needs both vitamins and fresh air! The ideal medium for fermentation is pure grape juice, which contains all the nutrients, or foods, that the yeast requires, but some of the liquors we ferment for country wines (notably mead and all the flower wines) are deficient in them, and it is therefore wise to add a nutrient to give the yeast a "boost", the nitrogenous matter mentioned previously.

You can obtain several good proprietary yeast nutrients from trade sources, but if you are likely to be making wine regularly and in reasonable quantities it will pay you to make up your own. Buy a 250 gm. jar of ammonium sulphate B.P. $(NH_4)_2SO_4$ and one of ammonium phosphate $(NA_4)_3PO_4$ and use half a level teaspoon of each in each gallon of wine. This will provide all the nitrogen and phosphate that the yeast needs, and the chemicals will always be ready to hand in your cupboard.

The other invaluable nutrient which has a wonderful effect upon the vigour of a fermentation is Vitamin B_1, or thiamine, as you can quite easily prove for yourself by adding it to some trial gallons. Buy it as tiny tablets (3 milligram size) from your chemist (they are sold under various brand names, such as Benerva) and use them regularly at the following rates per gallon:

Fruit wines	**1 tablet**
Grain, root, leaf and vegetable wines	**2 tablets**
Flower wines	**3 tablets**

This addition of "nutrient" to the "must" does certainly enable the yeast to carry the fermentation just that little further, and is a great help in the production of strong, *dry* wines, and in the avoidance of oversweet wines.

Other good general purpose nutrients to have by you are potassium phosphate and magnesium sulphate. Often, too, plain malt extract (not the cod liver oil variety!) can be used advantageously at the rate of one dessertspoon per gallon to get a fermentation away to a vigorous start, but it is wisest to restrict this practice to red or dark, full-flavoured wines, since it will impair the flavour and colour of light, delicate ones.

Sugars

MANY old recipes advocate far too much sugar, with the result that the winemaker is disappointed when the yeast fails to use most of it up, and he is left with a syrupy, almost undrinkable concoction.

As a good rule of thumb, remember the figure 3; 3 lb. to the gallon of liquor for a medium wine. Half a pound less will usually produce a dry wine, half a pound more a sweet. Below 2 lb. of sugar to the gallon the wine may not be strong enough to keep, above 3½ it may well (although not always) be sickly sweet.

So remember—2½ lb., dry; 3 lb., medium; 3½ lb. sweet.

Or, per litre—250 gms., dry; 300 gms., medium; 350 gms. sweet.

Many old recipes, too, specify candy sugar, but this is a hangover from the days when most sugar was unrefined and this was the best quality obtainable. Nowadays there is little to choose, for all practical purposes, between modern refined beet or cane sugars; they are all of excellent quality. Brown or Demerara sugar will impart a golden colour to a wine. It is therefore sometimes used to colour an uninteresting-looking wine, but it should not be used with wines where one wishes to retain a delicate, natural colour from, say, a flower. It will also impart a slight flavour.

"Invert" sugar, too, is now available to winemakers. When yeast sets to work upon household sugar, or sucrose, it first splits it into its two main components, glucose and fructose, or "inverts" it. In "invert" sugar this has already

23

been accomplished chemically, so that the yeast can start immediately to use the glucose (the principal sugar found in grapes). Thus by using "invert" one may well obtain improved fermentation, improved to the extent that the yeast does not itself have to effect the inversion. "Invert" will ferment more quickly than household sugar, and is widely used in the brewing industry. If you wish to use "invert" sugar, use 1½ lb. or kilo in place of every one of household sugar specified in the recipes.

Pure glucose, or grape sugar, can also now be purchased; and 18 oz. of it will replace 16 oz. of sucrose; both this and "invert" are naturally slightly more expensive than ordinary domestic sugar. Honey, of course, can also be employed to produce mead-flavoured wines. With liquid honey or thick, crystalline honey use pound for pound.

It is a good idea, since it eases the task of the yeast and makes for better fermentation, to add the sugar in stages, half the total quantity at the outset, and the remainder by stages in 4 oz. lots each time the ferment slows.

Draw off a pint or so of the wine, dissolve the sugar in it by stirring thoroughly (use no heat or you will kill the yeast) and restore the sweetened quantity to the main bulk of the wine. Any undissolved sugar in the wine may cause the ferment to "stick".

A dry wine can always be sweetened, but there is little one can really do about a wine which is oversweet, other than blend it with a dry one of the same type. If you decide to sugar a finished wine and are afraid this may start it fermenting again, add one Campden tablet per gallon to prevent this occurring. Or you can use for the purpose one of the sweeteners such as Sorbitol, which are non-fermentable by wine yeasts and therefore cause no fermentation.

An excellent stabiliser is potassium sorbate, the use of which in wine was made legal in 1974. Use it at the rate of 1 gram. per gallon, adding it before bottling.

Getting the flavour

THERE are several ways of extracting the required flavour from our fruit or vegetables—pressing, using juice extractors, or boiling, soaking in hot or cold water, and fermenting on the "pulp"—and there are advantages to each; which one uses depends on the wine being made and the equipment available (which usually means how much one is prepared to spend!).

Sometimes one first extracts the juice from all the ingredients and starts the fermentation right away. The straight juice may be fermented, but for reasons of economy (to avoid using too large a quantity of fruit) and so as not to have too strong a flavour, it is more usual for the juice to be diluted with water.

Alternatively, the fruit is pulped, the "must" prepared, and the yeast introduced, so that the fermentation begins immediately, and the liquor is not strained from the solids until, say, 10 days later. This is more convenient for those who do not wish to buy the more expensive equipment. Whichever system is used, the quantities advocated in the recipes remain the same.

In the latter case it is a great help to extraction to add 1 teaspoon of a pectin-destroying enzyme such as Rohament P, Pektolase or Pectinol, to hasten the breakdown of the fruit (and, incidentally, ensure a clear wine). It should be added 24 hours before the yeast, and only when the "must" or juice is cool or cold. (Boiling water will destroy the enzyme.) For maximum *flavour* release Rohament P, which has a near-miraculous action, should be used at room temperature for up to 24 hours and for maximum *colour* release for 1–2 hours at 104°F. (40°C.). It is not, however, suitable for producing a clear juice, so for winemaking Pectinol should be used simultaneously or subsequently. Both preparations are used at the rate of 2.5 gms. to 6 lb. fruit; a tin-lid measure is supplied with Shirlett-brand packs.

Pressing: Ideal for grapes (which must first be broken), fruit and berries. Even if you cannot afford the luxury of a proper press—and they are not expensive now—it is well worth contriving one of your own or borrowing one from your winemaking club. I have found that the ideal combination for the serious winemaker is some sort of fruit crusher with which to mash the fruit, and a Loftus press with which to press it: these will deal effectively with almost anything, even, say, a hundredweight of apples.

25

Extractors: the modern way. Juice extractors can now be obtained quite cheaply and range from the simple, hand-operated one which is a development of the old-fashioned mincer to sophisticated, powerful electric models such as the Kenwood, Beekay and "Nature's Bounty". Of these I have used only the last regularly, and must say that this is wine-making de luxe. With most of the makes available one uses 1 or 2 lb. of fruit at a time. It is effortless, but the filter has to be cleaned out after every 4 or 5 lb. and this becomes tedious when doing larger quantities. The "Nature's Bounty" ejects pulp and juice separately, and is far more satisfactory, since it therefore does not clog so quickly.

Cheaper than these, or than a press, is a steam extractor, and this, like the others, will separate the juice from the pulp most efficiently.

Again, this is a really excellent system for dealing with smaller quantities of a few pounds of fruit or vegetables, and a real delight in that it is so clean and delivers sterile juice, but I find it rather slow and tedious if one wishes to handle larger quantities. This is because each time one reloads with fruit there is an appreciable delay before juice starts to run, even if boiling water is used.

Boiling (necessary with some root and fruit wines): is a method that has to be used with care, for if the ingredients (particularly parsnips and plums) are overboiled it may later prove difficult to get the wine to clear. The liquor is then strained off the solids, cooled and fermented.

Cold water soaking: the fruit is pulped or the "must" prepared, the yeast is introduced, and the liquor is not strained from the solids until, say, 10 days later. This can be used with hard fruit as a preliminary to pressing. All you really need is a large crock or dustbin.

Hot water soaking: boiling or near-boiling water may be poured over the ingredients, which are then left to soak for three or four days, the yeast having been introduced when the "must" has cooled to 70°F. (21°C.). The liquor is then strained off.

Where boiling water is used the "must" will have been purified, for any wild yeast which may have been present will have been killed, but if pressing or the cold water method

26

are employed it is as well to add one Campden tablet per gallon, and to wait 24 hours before adding one's chosen yeast. The sulphur dioxide of the tablet will dispose of unwanted wild yeasts but 24 hours later its action will have abated sufficiently to allow your selected yeast to start working satisfactorily.

When, by one of these means, the flavour has been extracted, the sugar is added and the yeast and yeast nutrient introduced in order to cause fermentation, and the fermentation is then conducted as described later.

Acidity

... plays a vital part in determining wine quality. Lack of acid will mean a poor fermentation, and a "medicinal" taste in the finished wine, which will also lack character and seem insipid. In any wine it is essential that acidity, tannin content and degree of sweetness should be "in balance" according to the type of wine being made (a sweet wine will need more acid than a dry). A quarter of the original acidity of a "must" disappears during fermentation (so that tasting one's "must" affords some guide) and a finished wine should have between 5 parts per thousand (dry) and 7 parts per thousand (sweet). This, in most recipes, will be obtained by adding the juice of one or two lemons, or $\frac{1}{4}$–$\frac{1}{2}$ oz. citric acid per gallon (10–15 gms. per 5 litres).

A simple way of testing the acid content of a wine or "must" is to use B.D.H. Narrow Range pH indicator paper (aim at a colour reaction equivalent to between pH3 and 4). This is not entirely accurate but it is probably enough for most of us.

Those wanting more precision should note that the desirable acidity of table wines, in terms of sulphuric acid, is from 4 to 6 grams per litre, according to type.

The only really satisfactory method of assessing acidity is by titration, and kits for this purpose can be bought for as little as £1. A graduated pipette is used to take a given quantity of the wine to be tested and this is run into a beaker. A piece of blue Litmus paper is added and this is immediately turned red by the acid present. A commercially-prepared potassium

27

hydroxide solution (11.43 grams of pure potassium hydroxide per litre, the equivalent of 10 grams per litre of sulphuric acid) is then carefully added, until the Litmus paper turns blue again. Note how much solution you have used and from the chart provided you can tell the acidity of the wine. Do three such tests and take the average.

Tannin

A small quantity of tannin will vastly improve the taste of most wines, giving them a zest or bite which is otherwise lacking, particularly in flower, root and grain wines. It is the tannin in a wine which gives an impression of dryness in the mouth after drinking; if the right amount of tannin is present, the wine will be supple and zestful; if too little, flat, insipid and characterless; if too much, harsh, astringent and bitter. Tannin is also an essential constituent if a wine is to have good keeping qualities.

Tannins come from the skins and stems of fruit—particularly red fruit, and wines made from all red fruit and from elderberries, bilberries, sloes, damsons, plums, apples, pears, grapes, and oak leaves are liable to be rich in tannin, and usually need none added. In flower and grain wines add one teaspoon of grape tannin, a few oak leaves or pear peelings, or one tablespoonful of strong tea per gallon. It is not really practicable for the amateur to test for tannin content.

Sometimes, particularly with elderberry wines, one has an excess of tannin. This is caused by using too much fruit, by soaking for too long a period, or pressing too hard. If a finished wine is a little too harsh, it can often be vastly improved by the addition of a little sugar or glycerine, but if it is far too harsh it should be fined with gelatine or blended with another softer wine.

Conducting your fermentation

NOW let us get on with the making of an orthodox country wine. If you are fermenting a juice, or a liquor with no solid ingredients left in it, it can well go straight into a fermenting jar which, however, should not be filled beyond the shoulder, and a fermentation trap fitted. (If you fill your jar the ferment, in its first vigour, will foam out through the trap.)

The yeast and yeast nutrient are added at the same time and the jar is placed in a warm place, about 70°F. (21°C.). A warm kitchen is ideal, but do *not* stand the jar on a stove or anywhere it is likely to be *over* heated, or the yeast may be killed, and fit either a cotton wool plug or an airlock. After four or five days or so the ferment will quieten, and the jar should be "topped up" to the bottom of the neck either with some of the liquor or with syrup of the same strength as the original liquor. The air-lock, of course, is again fitted.

The jar is then best kept at a temperature of 60–65°F. (16–16°C.) until fermentation is finished. Check it regularly, particularly if you are adding sugar by stages, and watch both specific gravity and the air-lock action.

When the ferment appears to have finished, move it back into a warm room for a few days to see if it restarts.

If you are dealing with a "must" with a large quantity of solid ingredients you will probably find that, at least for the first 10 days or so after the yeast has been added, because of the great bulk, it will probably be necessary to use a crock or polythene container such as a bucket or bin. This must be closely covered with several thicknesses of cloth or a sheet of polythene secured with elastic to keep vinegar flies at bay. Again . . . a temperature of 70°F. (21°C.). Do not forget to stir the "must" from the bottom twice daily.

At the end of the soaking period strain off the liquor through a nylon sieve or two or three thicknesses of muslin— do it thoroughly and do not hurry it—into your fermenting jar and fit your air-lock, carrying on thereafter as above.

Stuck ferments

IF you have used the right amount of sugar and fermentation has apparently ceased too soon (the wine will be oversweet and its specific gravity too high) the fermentation is said to have "stuck". Possible causes: Too high or too low a temperature; the yeast has reached its limit of alcohol tolerance (i.e., the wine is finished); the sugar has all been utilised (add more); too much sugar (dilute slightly); insufficient nutrient or acid (add more); insufficient oxygen (aerate by stirring and pouring); too much carbon dioxide (uncork and stir). If these and all other remedies fail, make up a half pint starter with the juice of three oranges, water, 1 level dessertspoon sugar, yeast, and a pinch of nutrient. Get it going well, then add an equal quantity of the "stuck" wine. When all this is fermenting, again add an equal quantity of the wine and continue "doubling up" in this way until all is fermenting once more.

Racking

ONE of the most important factors in producing clear, stable wine is racking, i.e., siphoning the wine off the lees of yeast and deposited solids; more wines have been ruined by neglect of racking than from any other cause. During the first fermentation a wine will be milky and soupy—and often downright repulsive!—in appearance, and no one would imagine that one day it will be brilliantly clear, and perhaps

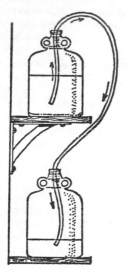

Left: The clean jar into which the wine is racked must be at a lower level. Start the siphon by sucking the end of the rubber tube.

Right: A more sophisticated syphon. The rubber tube is attached to the top of the glass tube, which can be pushed to any depth. Start by blowing on small tube. This syphon will not disturb sediment.

RACKING, OR SYPHONING

even sparkling. But do not dismay. Properly made, and properly managed subsequently, almost all wines will clear of their own accord. Some wines, parsnip and plum among them are notorious for their slowness to clear, and it should be noted that it is usually where the ingredients have been boiled that this occurs, for boiling releases pectin to cause hazes in the wine. These hazes, however, should not be confused with the thick cloudiness of the early stages of fermentation.

A wine is likely to remain really cloudy for three or four months after the fermentation is started because of the yeast in suspension; then, slowly, it will commence to clear, from the top down, as the yeast and solids in it sink to the bottom, forming a thick layer at the bottom of the fermenting jar. When the wine has cleared in this way—rack.

Place a clean jar below the level of the one containing the wine, and remove the bung and air-lock. Take a yard or so of acrylic tubing (about half an inch diameter) and in one end of it fit a foot of glass or other rigid tubing. Insert the tubing carefully into the wine (carefully so as not to distrub the sediment) to about half the depth of the jar, and hold it in place by clipping a wooden clothes peg around it, or by using a rubber band.

Take the lower end of the tube down to below the level of the bottom of the fermentation jar, put it into your mouth, and suck steadily (most pleasant, this!). When the wine is flowing freely direct it into the new jar. As the level in the fermentation jar drops push the glass tube down further and further until you have racked off all the wine and only the yeast sediment is left. Be careful not to siphon that into the new jar.

Before fitting the air-lock to your new jar of semi-clear wine, make sure that the jar is filled to the bottom of the neck, so that the minimum of air is allowed access to the wine.

Do this by "topping up" if necessary (and it usually is) with syrup, made to the same strength as your original "must". Thus, if your original "must" had 3 lb. of sugar to the gallon (48 oz.) use 3 oz. of sugar in half a pint of water.

Then insert your air-lock and allow the fermentation to

proceed again. At first it will probably be much slower than previously, but do not worry about this; it is because the quantity of yeast present has been greatly reduced. As the yeast gradually multiplies again so the ferment will get going once more, and a slow, steady ferment, rather than a fast one, is what you want.

The wine will also continue to clear, and the yeast will throw a second deposit. When the wine is *completely* clear, and the sediment is firm, comes the time for your second racking. This time "top up" with other wine, brandy or water and not with syrup or you may get an interminable fermentation. (The yeast left behind on this occasion will be an excellent medium for starting off other brews.)

You may care to bottle on this occasion, but it is preferable to give the wine yet a third racking after another two months before doing so. Normally about three months elapse between first and second rackings but it is impossible to give a firm schedule since the time to rack depends upon the progress of the individual wine.

Racking rarely harms a wine, and generally improves it; racking helps to stabilise the wine, thus reducing the risk of after-bottling fermentation and consequent burst bottles; racking also prevents the wine acquiring off flavours from the dead yeast upon which it would otherwise be standing.

Always make sure that your fermentation is completely finished before bottling, or you may have burst bottles, which is both messy and dangerous. Most beginners fall into the error of trying too bottle too soon, and pay dearly for their mistake. It always pays, for the same reason, to add sulphite at the rate of 50 p.p.m. (1 crushed Campden tablet per gallon) or potassium sorbate at the rate of 1 gram. per gallon before bottling. If you use potassium sorbate as a stabiliser, for which purpose it is excellent, note that one Campden tablet per gallon must also be used in conjunction with it, or the wine may acquire a "geranium" smell.

Clearing

NORMALLY a well-made wine will clear of its own accord, given time (which can be as much as a year in some cases) but when it does not, it may be necessary to resort to fining or filtering. The best advice that we can give, however, is: *always* give your wine a chance to clear naturally. Avoid fining, which may upset the chemical balance of the wine, and filter only as a last resort, for filtering does take something out of a wine besides the murkiness.

Usually all that is necessary is to move the wine, at the end of fermentation, into a much lower temperature (say from a warm kitchen to a cold larder or outhouse, but *not* into a refrigerator). In some case, if you have some clear wine of the same sort from the previous year, pouring some of this in on top of the new wine will rapidly clear it.

If your wine remains obstinately cloudy, you can try using filter paper of a coarse grade which should be folded in a series of vertical creases to present the maximum area to the wine. Fold your paper in halves, then quarters, then eighths; then unfold and refold it between the original creases, but the opposite way. It will then present a fluted appearance. A small plug of cotton-wool placed in the funnel before the filter will prevent a disaster if the bottom point of the filter paper gives way! Even ordinary tissues, used double or treble thickness, will provide a reasonable filter.

If these methods fail to work, it may be necessary to resort to fining. The commercial wine world uses several types, organic (gelatine, isinglass, egg whites, egg albumen powder, pure ox blood, casein, etc.), mineral (Bentonite, Kaolin or Kieselguhr) and vegetable (alkaline alginates), but some of these are risky in the hands of the amateur, since they require a reasonably exact dosage calculated as the result of experiments, and it is difficult to work down to the smaller quantities we usually need. Many proprietary wine finings work on the simple principle that tannins and proteins precipitate one another and therefore add in turn some of each.

Many prefer to play safe and buy some reliable proprietary finings, with detailed instructions.

Quite the best general-purpose finings that I have come across is Winecleer, sold by Homebrews Ltd., of Southampton, which I have found to have a startling effect in a wide range of both white and red wines not of sufficient clarity. It certainly seems to tackle most hazes, and the beauty of it is its ease of use: one merely adds between $\frac{1}{4}$ and $\frac{1}{2}$ fl. oz. per gallon (10–20 mls. per 5 litres) and then leaves the wine for a couple of days to clear.

Another excellent "general-purpose" way of clearing hazes from, and lending real clarity to, your wines is fining by means of BENTONITE ($Al_2O_3.4S_iO_2.H_2O$), an excellent clarifying and stabilising agent. A montmorillonite clay which can absorb ten times its own weight of water, with which it forms a gelatinous paste, it causes a coagulation of the proteins, which increases proportionately as the acidity of the wine is greater and the tannin content smaller, and its action appears almost miraculous.

It can be purchased from Semplex, Rogers (Mead) Ltd., Boots, and most other wine supplies firms, and should be used at the rate of $\frac{1}{4}$ oz. of Bentonite to 3 fl. oz. of water. (50 gms. to $\frac{1}{2}$ litre). Since it will keep indefinitely, but has to be made up at least 24 hours before use, it pays to make up a quantity at a time, and preferably to do so at the outset in two small containers, so that when one is used up it can be immediately replenished, and the suspension in the second container will have been standing for weeks, or even months, and will be ready for use.

Use 1 pint bottles with flat bottoms and screw caps; fruit juice bottles are ideal. Into each bottle pour 9 fl. oz. of water (boiled and then cooled) and then funnel in $\frac{3}{4}$ oz. of Bentonite. Screw on the cap and shake vigorously, impacting the liquid against the flat bottom of the bottle to force the Bentonite into suspension. Then leave the bottles for at least 24 hours, and preferably more, before use, to allow the montmorillonite particles to swell and become effective coagulators.

To use the suspension, remember that in each bottle you have $\frac{3}{4}$ oz. of Bentonite. The advocated dose for all ordinary hazes or straightforward fining is one-eighth of an ounce per gallon of wine, and for really bad hazes $\frac{1}{4}$ oz., so you will need to use one-sixth of the contents for "normal" fining, and one-third of the contents for really thick hazes. (Metric dose: 5–10 gms. per 5 litres.)

The wine should, of course, have been racked off any deposit. Draw off a little to make room for the suspension, measure out the "dose" of Bentonite, pour it into the wine through a funnel, and top up as required with wine. Re-cork, and then rotate or swirl the jar gently to mix the Bentonite into the wine. Keep it in suspension for at least 20 minutes by rocking and swirling at 3-minute intervals. Rack after a month, *not* before.

You may be looking for a method of not only fining your wines (i.e., removing any suspended solids or hazes) but of "polishing" them as well, bringing them up to that brilliance which makes them really attractive and will carry off the prizes when they appear on a show bench. For many years amateur winemakers employed *loose* asbestos pulp until there was a scare that this might be a health hazard and to be on the safe side I do not recommend its use.

They are far better advised to buy one of the superb proprietary filters now on the market, either the Harris filter, marketed by Rogers Mead Ltd., which coarse filters, fine filters and polishes by means of special powders, or the type of filter which employs a compressed disc or pad similar to those used in the commercial wine world, and which may contain little or no asbestos. The Vinbrite, for instance, marketed by Southern Vinyards of Brighton, uses a pad made of silicone fibres with a maximum of 12% asbestos content, the same medium as is used for the filtering of insulin for diabetics. Boots Ltd. sell a somewhat similar filter, and all three of these—Harris, Vinbrite and Boots—do a first class job on wines that are already reasonably clear; and they cost under £3.

But if you can spare a bit more cash, invest in a Vinamat (from Home Winemaking Supplies, Chichester) a really superb job which filters wine really rapidly under pressure through outsize pads, and will speedily clear the soupiest brews; it's a delight to use—but costs about £15.

Bottling

IT is better to use, if you can, true wine bottles since they show your wine off to better advantage. Be sure that

35

they have been sterilised, and always use new corks or stoppers (cork, NOT screw, stoppers).

Red wines, of course, should be put into dark bottles (except for exhibition or competitive purposes) or they will lose their glorious colour.

The bottles can be sterilised by means of the sulphite solution already described, and then drained; there is no need to dry them thoroughly internally. Many wine books warn against using "damp bottles", but this is only because people have been foolish enough to use bottles containing traces of moisture which may have been in them for a long time, which is not only unhygienic but asking for the wine to be spoilt by the bacteria which are inevitably present. A few drops of sulphite, on the other hand, can do no harm. The bottle should be filled to within three-quarters of an inch to the bottom of the cork.

Whichever kind of cork you use, soak it for 24 hours in cold boiled water beforehand to soften and swell it, then drive it right home. When using true wine corks, which are cylindrical in shape, a corking machine of some sort is a great help; without one it is difficult to force the cork in far enough. A cork "flogger" serves the same purpose (see page 7).

"Stopper" corks, with cork or wooden projecting caps, are favoured by many, because they lend themselves to use with an ornamental capsule, but they do not grip quite so tightly, and are apt to be forced out again by the pressure of the compressed air beneath them. To overcome this, put a length of thick string or pliable wire inside the neck of the bottle, leaving sufficient projecting to be able to grasp it firmly. Insert the cork and drive it home. Then, holding down the stopper with the thumb of the left hand, grasp the string or wire with the right, and pull it out. As it comes out it makes a path which the compressed air follows, thus leaving no pressure within the bottle. Whichever kind of cork you prefer, always try to use new ones (and never one which has been pierced by a corkscrew). If you *have* to use an old one, boil it first.

Some of the most popular stoppers of all nowadays are those made in polythene—winemaking suppliers stock them—

which can be used over and over again, and sterilised each time by boiling. They are neat, cheap, and ideal for the home winemaker, and allow bottles to be stored upright.

Finally, finish your bottle off with an appropriate label and coloured capsule of tinfoil or plastic to cover the cork. (It looks better if label and capsule match, and are of a suitable colour for the wine, red label for red wine, yellow for yellow, and so on.) On an ordinary wine bottle the label should be about a third of the way down the body of the bottle, i.e., the top of it should be about $1\frac{1}{2}$ in. below the shoulder, so that the main line of printing is in the "optical centre", and looks attractive. The label should be centrally placed between the seams of the bottle and not overlap them, or the appearance is spoilt.

Store your *bottles on their sides*, in a rack or bin if you can, and preferably in a temperature of about 55°F. (13°C.) in a place which is free of vibration and not brightly lit. Bottles with stopper corks are safer stored upright, because these are not as secure as full cylindrical corks.

The malo-lactic fermentation

OCCASIONALLY one comes across what is really a third fermentation, the malo-lactic fermentation. This occurs usually after the wine has been bottled, and often as much as a year or more after it was made. It is something which should be welcomed, when it does occur, for it imparts a very pleasant freshness to a white wine, and does reduce the acidity a little.

Malic acid is the acid to be found in apples, and what happens during the malo-lactic fermentation, as the name indicates, is that a bacterium to be found in all fresh wines (*b. gracile*) sets to work on the malic acid and converts it into lactic acid. This might not seem much of an improvement, but the lactic acid is much *less* acid than malic, and the acidity of the wine is thus reduced, to say nothing of the very pleasant, clean freshness with which this slight fermentation endows the wine, giving it a slight prickle or sparkle.

Occasionally, one can bring about such a fermentation

by agitating any yeast deposit and bringing the wine into the warm, but usually one can only be duly grateful if it occurs of its own accord!

Sparkling wines

A MALO-LACTIC fermentation will give you a sparkling wine accidentally, as it were, but it is even more fun to make one deliberately. All you need is a suitable "must"— apples, pears, gooseberries, rhubarb are all ideal ingredients— a champagne yeast, and not too much sugar (about $2\frac{1}{2}$ lb. to 1 gallon, or an S.G. of 1080–1085, giving a wine of about 10%). Ferment this to dryness, rack twice, mature for about six months, and then bottle in champagne bottles, adding to each 1 level teaspoon of sugar and a little fermenting champagne yeast. Cork well with a true cylindrical wine cork and wire it securely. Mature for at least three months. *Do not make this wine in ordinary wine bottles;* they will not stand up to the pressure involved.

If you wish to make an "instant" sparkling wine and are lucky enough to possess a Sparklet siphon you can do so in this way. First chill the wine in the refrigerator. With the plastic sleeve in position in the neck of the siphon, pour in the wine until it nearly reaches the top but do not top up if the level drops. Insert the siphon tube and firmly screw on the head. Charge the siphon with a Sparklets bulb in the usual way and shake vigorously. After this the siphon may be placed in a refrigerator if it is required to be cooled, but when it comes to dispensing, instead of discharging the wine through the spout, *turn the siphon upside down* so that the end of the siphon tube projects above the liquid, then with a napkin held over the spout to prevent splatter, depress the lever of the siphon until excess gas has been discharged. Turn the siphon upright again and unscrew the head. The wine may then be poured into glasses as if from a bottle by first removing the plastic sleeve from the neck of the siphon. However, always remember to replace the plastic sleeve before refilling. Hey presto!—Sparkling wine. An excellent book on the subject is *How to Make Sparkling Wines* by John Restall and Don Hebbs (75p, post 17p).

Winemaking summarised

1. Extract flavour.
2. Add sugar and yeast and ferment for up to 10 days in a bowl or crock, closely covered, at about 70°F. (21°C.). (This may be simultaneous with 1.)
3. Strain off, put into fermentation jar or bottle; fit air-lock. Fill to bottom of neck. Temperature: about 60°F. (16°C.). This fermentation will be much quieter and will proceed for some weeks.
4. Rack the cleared wine. Repeat this about two months later, and, usually, a third time after a further month. By then the wine should be quite stable, with no risk of burst bottles later on.
5. Bottle when the wine is about six months old. Store bottles, on their sides, preferably in a room of 55°F. (13°C.) temperature or below.

The hydrometer

If the fermentation trap is the winemaker's best friend, it is certainly run a close second by the hydrometer. A hydrometer is by no means essential to the production of good wine, but it is a great help, particularly if one is aiming at consistent results.

Many winemakers seem to fight shy of it, but in principle it is quite a simple device; by means of it one can:

(a) determine how much sugar there is in any natural juice or must;

(b) determine how much sugar to add to a juice to produce a wine of the desired strength;

(c) keep a check on the progress of a ferment; and

(d) calculate the strength of the finished wine.

The word hydrometer means "water-measurer", but in this instance it would be more accurate to call it a saccharo-meter, or "sugar-measurer", for the basic purpose of the instrument is to discover how much sugar there is in the liquor. Fermentation, as has been explained, involves the conversion by yeast of sugar into alcohol and carbon dioxide. If, therefore, we can discover how much sugar is used up

Making a typical country wine ~ Elderflower wine

① INGREDIENTS

¾ PINT OF ELDERFLOWERS
1 GALLON OF WATER
3 LBS WHITE SUGAR
½ LB RAISINS, OR ¼ PINT GRAPE CONCENTRATE, THE JUICE OF THREE LEMONS, YEAST, YEAST NUTRIENT.

② CUT OFF FLORETS AND PRESS DOWN LIGHTLY

③ PUT SUGAR, FLOWERS, RAISINS, OR CONCENTRATE, LEMON JUICE IN BOWL, POUR ON BOILING WATER, STIR, ALLOW TO COOL TO 70° F.

④ ADD WINE YEAST STARTER OR ONE LEVEL TEASPOON GRANULATED YEAST — AND YEAST NUTRIENT (VERY IMPORTANT!)

⑤ COVER CLOSELY WITH THICK CLOTH OR POLYTHENE, SECURED BY ELASTIC, LEAVE FOR 4 OR 5 DAYS IN TEMPERATURE OF 65-70° FAHRENHEIT.

stir daily!

CONTINUED

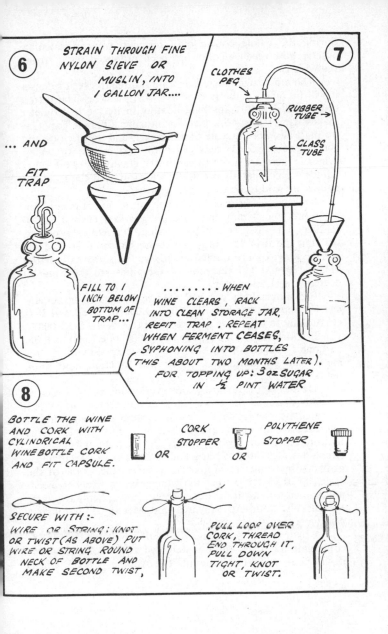

6 STRAIN THROUGH FINE NYLON SIEVE OR MUSLIN, INTO 1 GALLON JAR....

... AND

FIT TRAP

FILL TO 1 INCH BELOW BOTTOM OF TRAP...

7 CLOTHES PEG

RUBBER TUBE

GLASS TUBE

.... WHEN WINE CLEARS, RACK INTO CLEAN STORAGE JAR. REFIT TRAP. REPEAT WHEN FERMENT CEASES, SYPHONING INTO BOTTLES (THIS ABOUT TWO MONTHS LATER). FOR TOPPING UP: 3 oz SUGAR IN ½ PINT WATER

8 BOTTLE THE WINE AND CORK WITH CYLINDRICAL WINE BOTTLE CORK AND FIT CAPSULE.

CORK STOPPER

OR

POLYTHENE STOPPER

OR

SECURE WITH:- WIRE OR STRING: KNOT OR TWIST (AS ABOVE) PUT WIRE OR STRING ROUND NECK OF BOTTLE AND MAKE SECOND TWIST.

PULL LOOP OVER CORK, THREAD END THROUGH IT, PULL DOWN TIGHT, KNOT OR TWIST.

during the whole course of a ferment, we can calculate exactly how much alcohol has been produced, how strong the wine is.

The more sugar there is in a liquid, the thicker or denser it will become, or the greater its *gravity* will be. The better, too, it will support anything floating in it; the hydrometer makes use of this principle. To measure different gravities, we naturally need a scale of some sort, and an obvious and convenient standard from which to start is that of water. Water is therefore given the arbitrary gravity of 1,000, other liquids are compared specifically with this, and the resultant figures are said to be their *specific gravities*.

Thus liquids heavier than water (or, in our case, containing more sugar) may have *specific gravities* such as 1.050 1.120 or 1.117 degrees. When talking of gravities, however, we omit the first "1" and the decimal point. Therefore the *specific* gravities are quoted exactly as the same as *gravities* of 50, 120 and 117 respectively. Gravities are the same as degrees Gay Lussac (deg. G.L.).

For winemaking you will need hydrometers, or perhaps one hydrometer, covering the range 1.000 to 1.160 and it is often useful to be able to go several degrees below the 1.000.

If you wish, buy three, one 900–1.000, one 1.000 to 1.100 and one 1.110–1.200. You will then be equipped with hydrometers the graduations of which will be larger and more readable.

Messrs. W. A. E. Busby, however, produce one which is specially designed for the winemaker and which allows one to calculate the strength any wine has attained without reference to tables or graphs, which is most useful. This hydrometer has the specific gravity and the potential alcoholic strength scales side by side, and it costs no more than an ordinary hydrometer. Moreover, it covers the whole of the scale, 0.990 to 1.170, that the winemaker is likely to need, and is therefore ideal for our purpose, Boots, Semplex, Peter Stevenson's, Southern Vinyards and Messrs. H. T. Ellaway also have specialised models.

A hydrometer is a glass tube (with a bulbous lower end) containing the scale, and it is weighted at the bottom so that it will float upright in a liquid. The reading is taken where the level of the main surface of the liquid would cut the scale.

The thinner the liquid (the less its gravity) the deeper the hydrometer will sink in it; the denser the liquid (the greater its gravity) the higher the hydrometer will float, and the more of the scale will protrude above the surface.

Therefore the scale of figures in the hydrometer is "upside down", the smallest being at the top and the largest at the bottom. In water, of course, the hydrometer will float with the 1.000 mark level with the surface; as you add sugar so the hydrometer will rise in the liquid. If, on the other hand, you add instead to the water a liquid *lighter* than water—alcohol, for instance—the hydrometer will sink *below* 1.000.

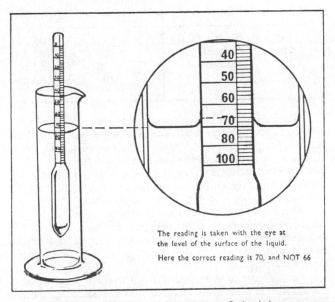

The reading is taken with the eye at the level of the surface of the liquid.

Here the correct reading is 70, and NOT 66

To use your hydrometer, pour some of the juice or syrup to be measured into a hydrometer jar, or any transparent container that gives sufficient depth and simple side clearance.

43

(A Drake trial tube will enable you to do this without disturbing your wine). Spin the hydrometer to get rid of any air bubbles clinging to its sides, which can seriously affect the reading. When the hydrometer is still, take the reading, with the eye at surface level.

Note that the hydrometers are designed to be read when the liquid is at 59°F., and, strictly speaking, if it is at any other temperature, you should allow for it as shown in the following table. Omit the "decimal point" of the specific gravity and make the correction to the last of its four figures. Example: A hydrometer reading of 1140 at 86°F. should be corrected to 1143.4.

Temperature Deg. F.	Correction	Temperature Deg. F.	Correction
50	Subtract 0.6	77	Add 2
59	Correct	86	Add 3.4
68	Add 0.9	95	Add 5
		104	Add 6.8

When you have measured the specific gravity of your juice or liquor, you can tell from the table overleaf firstly how much sugar per gallon it contains, and secondly, how much alchohol (in terms of the percentage of alcohol by volume) it is likely to produce, i.e., you can assess its potential alcoholic strength. This, remember, on the assumption that the wine ferments right out, and that all the sugar is used up.

There may be some obscuration, or unavoidable inaccuracy, at either end of the scale, caused by solids initially, and alcohol finally, but these figures give a practical working basis, and a deliberately conservative estimate of potential alcohol.

Let us assume that you wish to make a wine using a diluted fruit juice. Having extracted the fruit juice and diluted it with water as required, take the S.G. of it. Let us assume that you obtain a reading on the hydrometer of 1.040. This means, if you look at the table for a moment, that there is already 1 lb. 1 oz. of sugar present in the natural juice and that if you fermented it you would finish up with a dry wine of 5% alcohol by volume. This would probably not keep (under 10% it cannot be guaranteed).

So now you have to decide how strong a wine you wish to make. One can of course make a weak wine of, say, 5%, but it would have to be drunk young, and most winemakers

S.G.	Potential % alcohol by volume	Amount of sugar in the gallon		Amount of sugar added to the gallon		Volume of 1 gallon with sugar added	
		lb.	oz.	lb.	oz.	gal.	fl. oz.
1010	0.9		2		2½	1	1
1015	1.6		4		5	1	3
1020	2.3		7		8	1	5
1025	3.0		9		10	1	7
1030	3.7		12		13	1	8
1035	4.4		15	1	0	1	10
1040	5.1	1	1	1	2	1	11
1045	5.8	1	3	1	4	1	13
1050	6.5	1	5	1	7	1	14
1055	7.2	1	7	1	9	1	16
1060	7.8	1	9	1	11	1	17
1065	8.6	1	11	1	14	1	19
1070	9.2	1	13	2	1	1	20
1075	9.9	1	15	2	4	1	22
1080	10.6	2	1	2	6	1	23
1085	11.3	2	4	2	9	1	25
1090	12.0	2	6	2	12	1	27
1095	12.7	2	8	2	15	1	28
1100	13.4	2	10	3	2	1	30
1105	14.1	2	12	3	5	1	32
1110	14.9	2	14	3	8	1	33
1115	16.6	3	0	3	11	1	35
1120	16.3	3	2	3	14	1	37
1125	17.0	3	4	4	1	1	38
1130	17.7	3	6	4	4	1	40
1135	18.4	3	8	4	7	1	42

45

prefer to make table wines, which are usually of about 10–12% alcohol, or stronger wines of up to 17%. For wines above the latter strength, say for drinking *after* a meal, one must resort to fortification.

Say you decide to make a wine of 16% alcohol. The table shows you that this will require an initial S.G. of 1120, or a sugar content in the gallon of 3 lb. 2 oz. You already have 1 lb. 1 oz., so that you need to add 2 lb. 1 oz. of sugar and make the quantity up to 1 gallon, with more juice of the same dilution. Alternatively, if you wish to add sugar *to* a gallon of diluted juice which has a SG of 1040, and arrive at an SG of 1120, you need to obtain a further 80 degrees of gravity. This you can do by reading off the amount to add to one gallon against the SG of 1080, and you will see that you will end up with a volume of 1 gal. 23 oz. (not the 1 gal. 37 oz. opposite SG 1120). (This is because the original sugar was *in* the gallon and not added *to* the gallon). You can, of course, add all the sugar at the outset, as long as you ensure that it is thoroughly dissolved, and, if you then check with your hydrometer, the S.G. should be in the region of 1.120. Add a little of the sugar at a time to be on the safe side, testing as you go. A simple approximation is that 2¼ oz. sugar will usually raise the S.G. of 1 gallon by 0.005 (5 degrees).

You then add your yeast nutrient and ferment in the usual manner.

As the ferment proceeds the S.G. of the liquor will drop, rapidly at first, and then more slowly, and you can gain a good idea of its progress by noting the rate of drop. As it nears the 1.000 mark it will be very slow indeed. It may reach the 1.000, and may well drop below because of the presence of alcohol, in which case congratulate yourself upon having produced a really dry wine!

To calculate the final strength of the wine, write down (omitting the decimal point) the S.G. at the start of the ferment (i.e., after the sugar was added). Subtract from it the final S.G., and divide the answer by 7.36; that is the percentage of alcohol by volume of your wine.

Multiply that by 7 and divide by 4 and it will give you the strength as proof spirit.

Example: Starting S.G. 1125
        Final S.G... 1002
                                  ───
        Drop 123
                                  ───

$123 \div 7.36 = 16.7\%$ alcohol by vol.
Multiplied by 7-4ths = 29.2 deg. proof.

(To turn degrees proof into % alcohol by volume, one reverses the procedure, of course, i.e., multiplies by 4 and divides by 7.)

It is always good practice in winemaking to add the sugar by stages, but winemakers are often puzzled as to how they can do this, yet still use their hydrometer to obtain the information they want as to their wine's strength. It is easy enough if one bears in mind all the time that the principal factor with which one is concerned in calculating the final strength of a wine is the *total drop* in specific gravity. The sugar can therefore well be added a few ounces at a time *as long as you keep a record of the number of degrees drop between successive additions*. Then add up the various drops and this is the figure to be divided by 7.36 in the usual way. This will in normal cases give an approximate result which will be accurate enough for the average winemaker, but where large quantities of syrup are added it can be seriously adrift because it takes no account of the volumes involved. When you have worked out what percentage of alcohol you have obtained by the first drop, you then proceed to add sugar or syrup. This produces more alcohol, but its bulk also dilutes the alcohol you have already produced, so you must modify the calculation already done. Similarly the drop from the second lot of sugar must be modified, and so on.

Suppose you start with an S.G. of 1100 and, after three or four days, strain into a one-gallon jar and obtain 5 pints of liquid. Some time subsequently the S.G. is found to be 1000, i.e., a drop of 100. Since a gallon is required you "top up" these 5 pints, bring them to 7½ pints with an S.G. of 1010. After another period the S.G. drops again to 1005, so once more you top up with syrup or sugar to obtain a full 8 pints with an S.G. of 1010. The S.G. finally drops to 1005.

Using the rough-and-ready calculation above gives a

total drop of $100+5+5=110$. This one divides by 7.36, giving a result of 15% alcohol by volume.

But the correct calculation would be:

First drop: 100.

This must be modified into:

$$100 \times \frac{5 \text{ (the number of pints before topping up)}}{7\frac{1}{2} \text{ the number of pints after topping up)}}$$
$$= 100 \times \tfrac{2}{3} = 66.6$$

Second drop: 5.

Added to modified first drop$=66.6+5=71.6$. This again must be modified due to the second addition of sugar, as follows:

$$71.6 \times \frac{7\frac{1}{2}}{8} = 67$$

Final drop: 5.

To this 67 is added the final drop of 5, giving a total effective drop of $67+5=72$. This represents just under 10% alcohol by volume, as against 15% by the crude method.

Admittedly this is an exaggerated case and does not illustrate good winemaking practice, but it does illustrate the mathematical point.

A good general rule is that a really dry wine will often need a starting specific gravity of about 1.085, a medium sweet wine one of about 1.100, and a really sweet wine one of up to 1.125.

Always remember that it is better to use too little sugar initially than too much; a dry wine can always be sweetened; an oversweet wine is hard to redeem. Make your wines dry, and sweeten them to taste when finished.

Another useful point to note is that if you wish to *reduce* the gravity of a liquid, it can be done by dilution. The addition of an equal quantity of water, for instance, will reduce the gravity by half.

PEARSON SQUARE

SOMETIMES you will want to fortify a wine (raise its alcoholic content by adding spirit) and, since spirit is expensive, you will need to calculate exactly how much to add to achieve the desired result. Do so by means of the Pearson Square (or St. Andrew's Cross), but note that all measures must be of the same sort, i.e., degrees Proof or % alcohol by volume; do not mix them.

Here is the Pearson Square:

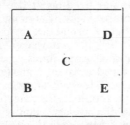

A=alcohol content of spirit to be added
B=present alcohol content of wine
C=desired alcohol content
D=difference between B and C
E=difference between C and A

The proportion D to E is the proportion of spirit to wine to achieve the desired strength.

If you are blending two wines of known strength and wish to know the final strength, the formula is:

$$\frac{(A \times B) + (C \times D)}{A + C} \text{ where:}$$

A=No. of parts of 1st wine
B=Strength of 1st wine
C=No. of parts of 2nd wine
D=Strength of 2nd wine

Thus, if you blend two parts of a wine of 15% with three parts of a wine of 10% the result will be:

$$\frac{(2 \times 15) + (3 \times 10)}{2 + 3} = \frac{60}{5} = 12$$

or a wine of 12%.

Concentrates and kits

I MUST not forget to say a word about the grape juice concentrates which are now on the market and which are a real boon to the winemaker who is anxious to see results quickly, yet at a reasonable price. Grape juice concentrates, of course will make "true wine", at a price far below that of wine bought in a shop, and by using it one can avoid all the "cookery" aspect of making wine at home.

Consequently many people are by-passing the flavour extraction part of the hobby nowadays and making wine from these concentrated grape juices—red or white—which have merely to be diluted as required, and fermented; excellent wine can be produced in this way at a most reasonable price. It has the advantage, too, that it is ready for drinking much more speedily than the average country wine, so that by using this system one can acquire cheaply the nucelus of a cellar whilst waiting for one's country wines to mature.

One of the best concentrates on the market has a specific gravity of 1.325 (see: Using Your Hydrometer). Recipes for its use involve adding 2, 2¼, 2½, 2¾ or 3 parts of water to 1 part of concentrate, plus the juice of one lemon per gallon to the supply requisite acid, and fermenting. For even greater dilutions one adds some compensatory sugar, the biggest dilution recommended being 1 gallon of grape juice to 4 gallons of water and 8 lb. of sugar (plus 1 oz. Tartaric Acid). Yeast culture is supplied with the concentrate.

This works out more expensive than most country wines, but with an average dilution the wine will still cost only 10p a pint.

Many firms have produced attractive kits with full instructions to enable a beginner to make his first gallon with ease. Some firms, notably Vinamat, Festival, Southern Vinyards Ltd., Continental Wine Experts, and Boots have raised this to a high level of sophistication, and one can now buy kits for making delightful wines like recognisable commercial types—Hock, Burgundy, Sauternes, sherry, etc.—although by E.E.C. regulations they cannot now be advertised under such titles. It is only fair to say that the quality can vary great-ly, according to whose kit you use, and how well you follow the instructions. Some kits using concentrate once tended produce rather "lifeless" wines, which I found were greatly improved by blending in a little fresh fruit juice of a compatible type. Recently, however, manufacturers seem to be using better quality concentrates and to have improved their products enormously, and you can certainly use the aforementioned kits with confidence. With some you can have good, reasonably priced wine ready to drink in under a month!

Grape concentrate is perhaps even better used as an additive in fruit wine musts, to improve their vinosity. (This was the purpose of including ½ lb. or 1 lb. raisins—dried grapes—in old-time recipes). Try substituting ¼ pint grape concentrate for ½ lb. raisins, and include this much concentrate in every gallon of your wine; it effects a great improvement in flavour and is quite inexpensive. It is therefore a good idea to keep available both white and red varieties in your winery.

A quarter of a pint of ordinary concentrate can be substituted for ½ lb. raisins or for about 3 oz. sugar, but if the brand of juice is very highly concentrated (as, for instance, Hidalgo's) less will need to be used. (Similarly, if raisins are really "sugary", reduce the quantity used a little).

Herbs and flavours

A simple and quick method of preparing herb wines of many varieties is by the use of a standard basic recipe, such as a concentrate wine, with the addition of the necessary herbs or the herb flavour extracted into the water for making the wine by steeping the dried herbs or boiling the fresh herbs.

Particular attention should be paid to obtaining the maximum extraction of the flavours and qualities of the herbs. Two ounces of dried herb usually suffice (a standard proprietary pack costing 10 or 15p will meet your requirements) and certain herbs with strong aromatic qualities may be suspended in a linen bag for a few days in the liquor made from a standard basic recipe. Check from time to time until the strength of flavour is to your liking. An ordinary fruit and grain wine is also an excellent base; so is tea wine.

The herbs, powdered or bruised, can be either:

iled or soaked in the gallon of water and strained
re adding to the main recipe.

dded to the "must"; or

nded in a linen bag in the fermenting standard
"must".

..other development is the introduction of flavourings,
which can be used to produce from any *finished* wine several
quite different aperitifs, and French or Italian Vermouth.
Flavourings are also obtainable to produce liqueurs at home
—Cherry Brandy, Curacao, Green and Yellow Convent,
Kirsch, Eau-de-Vie, Juniper Gin, etc., etc. With liqueurs,
of course, some fortification with brandy or vodka is to be
recommended, to obtain the strength required (liqueurs are
really sweetened spirits). Some economy can be effected by
using a proportion of strong wine in place of a third of the
amount of spirit recommended by the suppliers. Good books
on the subject are *Making Wines Like Those You Buy* and
How To Make Inexpensive Liqueurs.

In quantity

SOONER or later, most winemakers are not content to
make just one gallon of their favourite wines; their thoughts
turn to the idea of making them in larger quantities, say
4½, 5 or 6 gallons, or even more.

Many winemakers make 20 or 30 gallons of their
favourite wine each year and this "bulk" method has much
to commend it. Many winemakers are nervous of attempt-
ing, say, five gallons of one wine, but it is a fact that five
gallons is much less liable to "go wrong" than one, if ordinary
precautions are observed.

And consider the advantages . . . wine seems to ferment
better in bulk (in small quantities it is like a plant in too
small a pot!); the large bulk means that it is less subject to
violent temperature fluctuations; it is very little more trouble
to make five gallons than to make one (and it lasts nearly
twice as long!). Certainly, if you have a good stock of wine,
bolstered by one or two wines made in quantity, there is
less temptation to drink wine which is immature, and you
can still do your experimental single gallons.

By making a few wines in bulk you can have as much wine to drink as you wish, every day . . . a satisfying thought.

The way to set about it is to choose one or two ingredients which are readily available, or very cheap, and which can be relied upon to give you a wine of reasonable quality for your *vin ordinaire*, both red and white.

I personally have settled for apple for the white (from which a whole range of wines can be produced), and dried bilberry for the red.

The apple I make on the principle of 12 lb. of mixed apples to 1 gallon of water, which gives $1\frac{1}{2}$ gallons of "juice". (Metric: 5 kilos apples to 5 litres). Twelve pounds of apples fill a plastic bucket (an easy measure) and are run through a Bryants crusher, the resultant "purée" falling into an 11 gallon dustbin. Then a gallon of cold water is added. Then another 12 lb. of apples, another gallon of water, and so on. When I have enough a vigorous yeast is added and well stirred in. Do not forget adequate yeast nutrient. Fermentation on the pulp goes on for a week, the "cap" of fruit which rises to the top being broken up and well stirred each day.

Then the must is pressed and the juice runs off through a fine sieve into 1-gallon jars for measuring purposes. For each jar $2\frac{1}{2}$ lb. of sugar (for a dry wine) or 3 lb. (for a sweet) are put into a large bin, and all the 1-gallon jars emptied on to it. Then one stirs well to dissolve all the sugar before pouring all the "must" into a cask or carboy for the main fermentation—and the wine is made (Metric: $1\frac{1}{4}$–$1\frac{1}{2}$ kilos per 5 litres).

Apples are usually readily obtainable free in our area and we use a couple of hundredweight each year.

Dried bilberries, on the other hand, may sound expensive if one uses them at the rate usually recommended, 1 lb. to 1 gallon, but this is, if anything, too much. In practice, by successive mashings, one can get no less than 4 gallons of wine off 1 lb. of dried bilberries, the first gallon being of heavy body and the succeeding mashes each producing an increasingly light wine, the last being only a pale rosé. These four grades of wine enable one to blend to produce a wine of exactly the desired body and colour, and are excellent for blending with concentrate wines to produce further variety.

I now use 5 lb. of dried bilberries to 8 gallons of boiling water, 20 lb. of sugar, and five *level* teaspoons of citric acid. (Metric: 2½ kilos fruit, 35 litres water, 9 kilos sugar). The water is boiled in an electric boiler and run straight on to the ingredients. When it cools, add the yeast, and ferment for a week. Strain off the fruit and put on one side; run the liquor into fermenting casks, but put the last half-gallon aside in a glass jar stoppered with cotton-wool.

Return the fruit to the fermenting tun, run in five gallons of boiling water and a further 12½ lb. of sugar and three level teaspoons of citric acid. When this has cooled pour in the half-gallon from the previous must as a starter and it will almost explode into fermentation. The second batch is also fermented for a week before straining off the pulp and there will *still* be colour in the skins of the bilberries and goodness in the fruit to make a third batch if desired. This is an easily made winter wine and to my mind the colour and flavour of the bilberry is infinitely to be preferred to the more commonly made elderberry. *Bottled* bilberries from supermarkets are still quite cheap, and can be used in the same way.

Utensils for making wines in quantity are an ideal brewing boiler such as the Bruheat marketed by Ritchie Products, or any gas or electric boiler holding, say, 5 gallons. All we need it for in winemaking, of course, is boiling up large quantities of liquid but the Bruheat has the added advantage that it is equipped with a thermostat, most useful in holding a beer mash at a critical temperature when brewing beer. A large brewing bin, 11-gallon size, is useful, so is a fruit crusher to avoid having to cut up large quantities of fruit. A press you can do without at a pinch, and use pectin-destroying enzyme to break down the fruit instead. A wooden paddle is useful for stirring, so is a plonker for pushing down the cap of fruit during mashing. Both these are easily made from broom handles and squares of oak.

Containers for fermenting and storage? Carboys (fragile, but all right if you keep them in their rather untidy cages), stoneware "barrels" (old fashioned and heavy), plastic bags in cardboard outers (suitable but not very long lasting) and rigid polystyrene 5 gallon cubes. Of the last, those in which wines have been sold are usually safe, but others can confer horrible flavours upon your wine, even when they smell sweet, and are best treated with suspicion.

They should always be thoroughly washed out several times with boiling and cold water, be rinsed out with industrial alcohol (or cheap, sound wine), and be stored with a little sulphite in them. When used the first time, they should be filled with an inexpensive wine; if that survives untainted for a few months you know the container is safe for your more expensive wines.

My rule of thumb on storage, therefore, is: Use glassware, stoneware or casks whenever available, use plastic only if unavoidable, and test it before you trust it!

Casks

IF you have the time to look after them and the wine they contain, and can get them, casks are excellent; they are safe, easy to handle, long lasting and do impart "character" to a wine, but unfortunately they are increasingly difficult to obtain. Optimum sizes for home use are probably the $4\frac{1}{2}$ gallon and 6 gallon sizes, a 3 gallon being rather too small and a 9 gallon heavy to move. Paradoxically, the larger a cask is, the cheaper it is proportionally.

A few golden rules: Avoid like the plague casks which smell of vinegar. Keep your cask on a stand or stillage, so that the centre bottom stave is not supporting all the weight; **always keep casks FULL** (most important), topping them up regularly; refill a cask as soon as it is emptied; avoid the use of taps (which always drip and leak) and siphon wine out through the bung hole. Use always oak casks, wine casks if possible (beer "barrels" are thicker). Siphon wine into 1-gallon jars or bottles for drinking and refill cask. Normally keep separate casks for white and red wines.

TO PREPARE NEW CASKS: Fill with clean water for 2 or 3 days, then with hot soda solution (4 oz. soda in 1 gallon of boiling water). Rinse with sulphite solution ($\frac{1}{4}$ oz. potassium metabisulphite and $\frac{1}{2}$ oz. citric acid in 1 gallon water) and then with water.

55

TO STERILISE SECONDHAND CASKS: Fill with solution of hypochlorite (4 oz. of domestic bleach in 10 gallons of water). Leave 24 hours. *Or* half fill with hot soda solution as above. Roll, empty when cool. In either case then rinse (i) with water, (ii) with sulphite solution, and (iii) with water. (To remove surface deposit insert 3 foot length of heavy chain and roll cask.)

MUST SMELLING CASKS: Use $\frac{1}{8}$ oz. of calcium chloride, $\frac{2}{3}$ oz. sulphuric acid and 5 pints of boiling water. Leave 2 hours. Rinse with 10% solution of sodium hydroxide, then thoroughly with water.

STAGNANT SMELLING CASKS: Wash with 2 gallons of boiling water and 1 oz. of calcium chloride. Rinse with cold water.

STORAGE: Wash thoroughly, removing all surface deposit with chain, sterilise with sulphite solution. Some of this (say $\frac{1}{2}$ gallon for a $4\frac{1}{2}$ or 6 gallon cask) should be left in the bunged up cask. Store cask on end; invert at intervals; renew solution every two or three months.

Chamber of horrors!

FAULTS AND REMEDIES

WHILST something must be said about faults and diseases of wine, it should be emphasised at once that several of these disasters which can befall your wines are rarely encountered. Observance of commonsense precautions will ensure that your wines are sound, and you may never need to refer to these particular pages. I hope you do not!—but "just in case" there are listed here some of the disasters most probable to be encountered.

ACETIFICATION . . . or formation of vinegar. This will normally only occur in conditions of extremely bad storage, and in the presence of air. Therefore keep your bottles full. If it is noticed in the early stages—there is a very slight smell of vinegar and an acid taste—it can probably be halted by adding one Campden tablet per gallon, waiting 24 hours, and then introducing a vigorously fermenting fresh yeast. In the later stages the smell of vinegar will be pronounced, and indeed what you have now *is* wine vinegar. Remedy: Use it for cooking or pour it down the drain!

Sometimes a wine will smell vinegary but not taste acid, and this is the effect of ethylacetate, produced by wild yeast present on the fruit. Prevent this by adding one Campden tablet per gallon 24 hours before your chosen yeast.

OVER-SWEETNESS. The bugbear of the beginner. It can be avoided by not using too much sugar initially and always using a nutrient (see pp. 22 and 23). Remedy: Blend the wine with one from similar ingredients which is over dry, or with dry rhubarb wine, which will take up its flavour. See also "Low Alcohol Content".

LOW ALCOHOL CONTENT. Usually allied to over-sweetness. If it is the result of a fermentation having ceased prematurely, adding fresh yeast direct will rarely succeed, since it will be inhibited by the alcohol present. Remedy: Make up half-a-pint of fresh juice with 1 oz. of sugar and some fresh yeast and nutrient as a "starter". When it is fermenting vigorously add an equal quantity of the low-alcohol wine. When all is fermenting well, again add an equal quantity of the wine, and continue the process until the whole is fermenting once more. Adding nutrient to the bulk and keeping in a temperature of 70°F. (21°C.) will help.

OVER-ACIDITY. A slight over-acidity can often be corrected by stirring up any yeast deposit and causing a malo-lactic ferment. With a strong wine slight dilution will help to reduce acidity, and with a weak, dry one the over-acidity can often be masked (but not *corrected*) by the addition of a little sugar or by adding glycerine at the rate of 5%, or 1 pint to 2½ gallons. Do not exceed this. BEST REMEDY: 9 oz. of potassium carbonate made up to 1 pint with water. ½ fl. oz. of the solution reduces the acidity of 1 gallon by 1 p.p.t., without sediment or flavour change.

MEDICINAL FLAVOUR. The result of insufficient acid in the "must". If the fault is but slight the addition of a little citric acid to the finished wine may help, but if the flavour is pronounced little can be done.

MUSTINESS. Usually caused by standing overlong on baker's yeast or by musty casks.

MOUSINESS. Perhaps a corruption of the French wine term "moisi" or mouldy. This term refers to a smell rather than a taste (who has tasted a mouse, anyway?) which is very distinctive and pervasive. A drop rubbed in the palm of the hand will persist like perfume, but it's a foul odour of mice. No known cure.

TAINTS AND SMELLS. Not always readily identifiable; they can be caused by damaged fruit, bacterial action, tainted plastic containers, bad casks, or proximity of wine to strong smell (onion, paraffin, etc.). They can occasionally be removed by charcoal treatment but it is necessary to experiment to discover how much charcoal is needed. Add a small quantity to a measured quantity of wine, stir two or three times during the first 24 hours. Allow to settle. Leave a further day, then rack, and filter to remove particles of charcoal. Some of the flavour and colour may also be removed. If dose is satisfactory treat the bulk of wine in the same way.

METALLIC FLAVOUR. Sometimes encountered when wines have been made with tinned fruit, juice, or concentrate, or when ferrous metals have been allowed prolonged contact with the wine. Remedy: Avoid "unsafe" metals.

FAILURE TO CLEAR. Usually the result of over-boiling the ingredients (see "Pectin Hazes") or of hastening unduly the initial straining, which should be both slow and thorough. Remedy: Move wine into cold place for two or three weeks and see if it clears. If not, try filtering or Bentonite (see p. 34) or using a good wine finings, such as Winecleer. If these fail, try pouring into the top quarter of the bottle some *clear* wine of the same variety. This will often carry down the suspended solids. Isinglass or gelatine as finings are tricky, and not recommended for the beginner.

PECTIN HAZES. Many hazes in wines are due to gelatinous solutions formed by pectins in fruits, and are aggravated by initial boiling. They can be avoided by using a pectin-destroying enzyme such as Pektolase or Pectinol. To improve the yield of juice when making fruit, wines, the euzyme should be added to the pulp of the fruit, using $\frac{1}{2}$-teaspoon (2.5 gms.) to each 6 lb. pulp (a measure is supplied). If the juice is allowed to stand at room temperature overnight or longer the enzyme will act satisfactorily, and the juice will clear.

A check that any haze is caused by pectin can be made

by adding 3 or 4 fluid ounces of methylated spirit to a fluid ounce of wine. If jellylike clots or strings are formed, then the haze can be regarded as pectin and the remaining wine treated with Pectinol. For each gallon of wine 1 teaspoon (5 gms.) of Pectinol should be added to $\frac{1}{2}$ pint of wine and the wine kept warm (70–80°F., 21–27°C.) for four hours, stirring at intervals. Strain through muslin and add to the bulk of the wine. Leave the wine at 60–70°F. (16–21°C.) for several days. The pectin haze should clear, but if it does not try Bentonite.

STARCH HAZES ... can be treated with another enzymatic preparation, Fungal Amylase 2209 (10%). Starch is also sometimes present in unripe apples and should be removed before processing. The presence of starch can be detected by the removal of a small quantity of the material to be treated and the application of a drop of dilute iodine solution (afterwards, of course, discarding the portion tested). Even slight traces of starch will produce an unmistakable intense blue colouration. The enzyme is active at normal room temperature and in both finished wines and fruit juices. Use at the rate of $\frac{1}{2}$ teaspoon (2.5 gms.) per 5 gallons (20 litres) or 20 lb. (9 kilos) of fruit.

OTHER HAZES. Fine with Bentonite at the rate of $1\frac{1}{2}$ oz. to 10 gallons (see p. 00). Prepare a suspension of the necessary amount in a little of the wine, carefully breaking down all lumps; allow to rest for about two hours (and preferably 24), stir into the wine and stir several times during the first half-hour. Leave for up to one week, then siphon off clear wine from the sediment.

COLOURED HAZES. Usually the result of metallic contamination, copper, zinc and iron being the usual causes. Containers or implements of these metals should be rigorously avoided for fermentation purposes or white, dark, purplish or brown hazes may appear, often after a sudden drop in temperature, which renders the solutes less soluble. Remedy: For iron or copper hazes add a little citric acid; this often works.

DARKENING ... is most commonly caused by *oxidation*. If a glassful of finished wine darkens after 24 hours exposure to the air it is not fully stable. If the cause is enzymatic darkening can be prevented by adding 2 Campden tablets

59

per gallon as a stabiliser. Darkening may also be due to the presence of iron, which can be corrected by the addition of a little citric acid ($\frac{1}{2}$ oz. to 5 gallons).

TOO MUCH COLOUR. If you wish to decolour a white wine use casein, 4 level tablespoons of Marvel (dried milk) per gallon; allow to stand 24 hours, then syphon off sediment. This works wonderfully well, but not on oxidised white wine. You can alternatively try the charcoal treatment under "Taints and Smells".

HARSH FLAVOUR. Add glycerine to taste, or treat as for "Darkening", or use gelatine finings (see "Clearing", p. 32).

FILTER PAD FLAVOUR. Caused by failing to wash the filter pad with water or wine before filtration. The first wineglassful of wine through the filter should always be thrown away.

FLATNESS OR INSIPIDITY. The result of insufficient tannin in the wine. Remedy: Add grape tannin or a small quantity of strong tea (up to 1 tablespoon per gallon).

THINNESS, or lack of "body". Due to using insufficient fruit as the basis of the wine. Naturally thin wines, such as plum, can be improved by adding up to 1 lb. of wheat, barley or maize to the gallon when making. Thinness in a finished wine can only be overcome by judicious blending with one of considerably more body. Banana wine and robust grain wines are excellent for this purpose, since they usually have a good body. Regularly using a Campden tablet per gallon in the "must" 24 hours before adding the yeast will also improve the wine by putting into it a little glycerine.

FLOWERS OF WINE. Powdery, whitish flecks appear on the surface of the wine and if left unchallenged will rapidly increase and will turn your wine first into carbon dioxide and then to water. It is caused by an organism like yeast, mycoderma, an aerobic bacterium, and is usually the result of admitting too much air to the fermenting vessel. Remedy: Remove as much of the surface flecks as possible, filter through unmedicated cotton-wool or filter papers, introduce some vigorous fresh yeast, and fill the fermenting bottle as full as possible to exclude all air. If a substantial film has been formed there is no remedy.

ROPINESS. The wine takes on a repellent, oily appearance, and pours very slowly, like treacle, but the taste is unaffected. The wine will look rather like the raw white of an egg and in it will appear rope-like coils—hence the name. This is the work of the lactic acid bacterium. Remedy: Whip the wine into a froth in a polythene bucket, add two crushed Campden tablers per gallon, and filter.

Do

Keep all your equipment spotlessly clean.
Keep your first ferment closely covered.
Keep air away from the secondary fermentation.
Always use fermentation traps.
Keep all bottles full to within $\frac{3}{4}$ in. of cork.
Strain liquor off "must" slowly and thoroughly.
Make wines too dry rather than too sweet: sugar them later.
Use yeast nutrient regularly, and reliable yeast.
Add sugar by stages. Keep detailed records.
Rack at least once, and preferably twice or thrice.
Taste the wine you are making, at intervals.
Always use new corks or stoppers, and boil old ones.
Keep red wines in dark bottles, or they will lose their colour.

Don't

Sell or distil your wine.
Allow a single vinegar fly access to your wine at any stage.
Use any metal vessel if the wine will be long in contact with it.
Use any tools or containers of resinous wood.
Omit to stir a must twice daily.
Use too much sugar initially.
Try to speed a fermentation by too high a temperature.
Be impatient; making wine takes time.
Let your wine stand on dead yeast or sediment.
Filter unnecessarily or too soon; most wines will clear of their own accord.
Put wine in unsterilised bottles or jars.
Bottle your wine whilst it is still fermenting.
Use screw-stoppered bottles.
Drink too much!

Grow your own grapes

"BUT surely you can't ripen grapes out of doors in this country?" This, with variations, is the common incredulous reaction one gets each time the subject of outdoor vine-growing is mentioned to the average Englishman.

Vines, so the popular belief runs, are delicate, temperamental things, hard to propagate, complicated to prune, and suitable really only for greenhouse culture, and even then only by an expert viticulturist. And even if one succeeds in growing some vines, declare the pessimists, in our climate it will be impossible to ripen the crop.

These fallacies are widely believed, even amongst amateur winemakers, yet are the opposite of the truth.

Vines *can* be grown successfully in the southern half of England, and in a reasonably good summer the grapes can be ripened (a really wet one admittedly produces problems). And when we get one of our really hot summers, as we do occasionally, the owner of a vine is a happy man indeed.

Vines were grown in southern Britain by the Romans (so this is no new idea!) and today there are over 300 small vineyards where experiments are once more being made in order to accumulate indigenous experience again. In Hampshire, East Anglia, Sussex, Kent and the Isle of Wight, size-able plantings have been made and the English viticulture is being re-born.

Of those 300 vineyards, 150 are commercial (they are not all in production yet) and 150 are private.

The truth is that the growing and training of vines is so straightforward that *all* who are interested in winemaking should try it; vines occupy little space, they can be planted at the back of flower borders, along fences, beside paths, or on a south-facing wall. They make ideal screens, and they interfere little with flower or salad crops, for they are deep- and not surface-rooting. They are as easy to grow as, say, raspberries and blackcurrants. If they are grown espalier fashion along a wire fence it is the work of a moment to throw mats or polythene sheeting over them to protect them from frost, or netting to prevent depredations by birds when the grapes ripen.

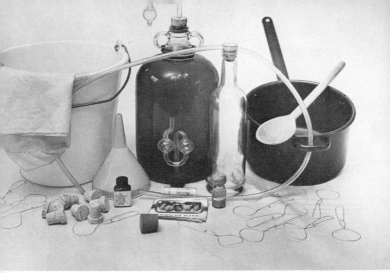

ABOVE: Minimum kit—plastic bucket and straining cloth, funnel, 1-gallon jar and fermentation lock, bottles, corks and wires, 1-gallon saucepan, polypropylene spoon, tube for siphoning, Campden tablets, yeast and nutrient.

BELOW: Useful chemicals—Campden tablets, ammonium phosphate, ammonium sulphate, potassium metabisulphite, bentonite, glycerine, sterilising fluid for glassware, Benerva Vitamin B_1 tablets, citric acid, wine tannin, and wine finings. Also shown is a cheap and useful balance for weighing small quantities and a set of measuring spoons.

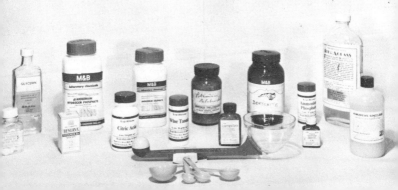

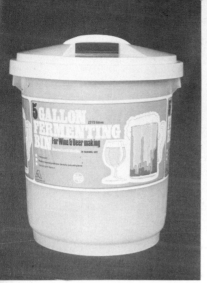

A popular and ideal 5-gallon fermenting bin and a useful bucket for the same purpose, fitted with tap, fermentation lock, and thermostatically controlled immersion heater.

BELOW and RIGHT: Boilers, a stainless steel saucepan and a thermostatically controlled Bruheat bucket.

PULPING FRUIT: For reducing fruit to a puree ready for easy pressing or fermenting the Pulpmaster is excellent. It consists of a stainless steel blade which fits any ordinary electric drill and which is slowly lowered into the fruit through a bearing in the lid.

Once the fruit has been crushed the juice can be extracted from it with a press such as this. It is run through a strainer into jars to facilitate measurement. Such a press is inexpensive to buy, or you can make your own. Other useful presses are shown below.

Yet another way of obtaining juice is by means of a steam juice extractor. The chopped fruit is placed in the perforated basket and hot water in the bottom chamber, and the appartus is then placed on the stove. The steam rises, breaks down the fruit tissue, and sterilised juice is drawn off the middle container.

Paul Stotler, of St. Albans, W. Va., U.S.A., with the simply constructed press he designed. Operated by a car jack, it is easily dismantled for storage by undoing half a dozen nuts and bolts. It will exert enormous pressure on the fruit, which is wrapped in strong hessian to make "cheeses", which are pressed between spacers made from battens. An ideal press for a Winemaking Circle.

Various large-scale fermenters. On the extreme right is an "ex-wine five" (gallons).

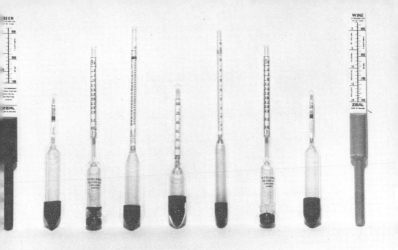

ABOVE: Several types of beer-brewing and winemaking hydro-meters. Saccharometer, or sugar measurer, would be a more accurate description.

BELOW: (right) The hydrometer reading is taken at eye level.
(Left) A refractometer, a much more expensive way of determining the sugar content of a must.

Fitting a 1-gallon jar with its bung and fermentation lock. An immersion heater is also fitted in this case, to hold the must at a pre-determined temperature to ensure a steady fermentation.

The all-important point is to make sure, when you choose your vines, that you select only the earliest cropping varieties. Just as the Englishman classes his potatoes as "First Earlies", "Second Earlies", "Maincrop", and so on, according to when the crop is ready, so the Frenchman talks of his vines as "Première Epoque", "Deuxième Epoque" or "Trois-pieme Epoque" (First, Second, or Third Epoch). Thus early ripeners are all of the "1ère époque", and very early ones the "1ère époque précoce". These will all ripen well in our English climate, whereas 2nd or 3rd Epoch vines will not. Black Hamburg, for instance, which is perhaps the most generally known grape in this country, is only so because it was once widely cultivated in greenhouses, but it is unsuitable for out-door use here, being of the Second Epoch.

Vineyards in the south of England are roughly the same latitude (49–50°) as Germany, where it is found that white grapes will ripen satisfactorily, but not red. Not surprisingly that has now been proved to be generally the case in England. So plump for an early-ripening, white, outdoor wine grape such as grown in Germany.

Those found most successful here have been Mueller-Thurgau (formerly known as Riesling-Sylvaner), Scheurebe, Seyve Villard 5276, Madeleine Angevine and Siegerebe. Others worth considering are Seibel 5279, Seibel 5409, Baco 2–16, Couderc 272–60, Chenin Blanc and Excelsior. If, despite the odds, you wish to try red grape varieties, go for Wrotham Pinot, Seibel 13.053, Pirovano 14, Baco No. 1 or Brant. Other "possibles" are Seibel 5455, 2010, and 8339, Seyve Villard 5–247 and Oberlin 595.

Consult your nurseryman, or better still a specialist vinegrower such as Cranmore Vineyard, Yarmouth, I.o.W., Jackman's Nurseries, of Woking, W. L. Cardy, Lower Bowden, Pangbourne, Berks., B. A. Theobald, Westbury Farm, Purley, Reading, Miss G. Pearkes, Rhyll Manor, Dulverton, Somerset, J. G. & I. M. Barrett, The Vineyards, Crocks Green, Felsted, Essex, J. R. M. Donald, The Garden House, West Tytherley, nr. Salisbury, Wilts, B. T. Ambrose, Nether Hall, Cavendish, Suffolk or A. Massell & Co. Ltd., Weare St., Ockley, Surrey. Many nurserymen can supply the more popular varieties.

It is not the intention to discuss here viticulture in detail, for many excellent technical books are available on the subject, but only to give, as it were, a few pointers to the complete novice. AW books on the subject that you will find a mine of information on the subject are: *Growing Grapes in Britain* by Gillian Pearkes (50p, postage 17p), *Growing Vines*, by N. Poulter, (60p, postage 14p) and *Wines From Your Vines* by the same author, (50p, postage 17p).

Firstly, if you are planting many vines, do not have all the same variety. Obtaining satisfaction from your vines will be a long-term project and it is best to choose several different vines and grow them experimentally rather than make a large outlay on one variety which may prove disappointing. Nor need this be expensive for cuttings from friends' vines can easily be rooted. Then select the ones that do best in your soil. Secondly, remember that vines fall into two main categories, producing wine grapes or dessert grapes, and that in each case black and white grapes of varying sweetness are obtainable.

So decide what type of grape you want, and choose some early burgeoning varieties to meet your need.

HYBRIDS

One point to note is that the beginner is well advised to plump for "hybrid" vines (Continental vines crossed with American) which are vigorous, prolific, early ripening and resistant to lime and disease. The American root stock resists the vine louse or (Phylloxera) which is the scourge of the *vitis vinifera*, or Continental varieties. The phylloxera kills off the vinifera by destroying the root system, but the American *vinis rupestris* stands up to it satisfactorily.

It is as well, too, to give your vine grower as much accurate information as you can about your soil, so that he can the better advise you.

You can either grow vines from cuttings or purchase them when 1–2 years old, and plant them in spring or autumn.

PLANTING

If you have them in a row or rows in the garden, growing on a waist high fence (which is a practical system because

64

they are then much more controllable and more easily protected) they should be at least 2 ft. 6 in. apart, preferably more, and there should be 3 ft. between rows.

When the vine arrives, if it has not been pruned, cut it down to the lowest two buds on each branch; even if it is 10 ft. high this *must* be done, or it will never grow grapes of any consequence.

The reason for this drastic pruning, and for those of subsequent years, is that for three years at least one should concentrate upon building up a really strong and extensive root system, and not top growth, otherwise the vine can never be really strong and prolific. Therefore the growth above ground must be curtailed so that all the strength of the plant will go into developing its roots. In the fourth year or is it is allowed to fruit. So vine-growing, as you can see is rather a long-term affair. Luckily winemakers are used to exercising patience!

Choose a sunny position for your vine, facing south if possible, dig a hole big enough to allow the roots ample room, and place the vine in position. Space out the roots well, and cover with light soil mixed with silver sand and old compost until the hole is filled. Be sure to tread well in.

As with raspberries, the fruit of the vine is borne on the wood of the previous year, so if a vine is spring planted you *could* obtain your first grapes in 18 months (though they will be scanty and it is better not to let the vine fruit). Certainly no more than two or three bunches should be allowed to form, or the strength of the vine will be sapped, but from then on a few more may be allowed each year until, in about four years, the vine will be cropping well.

As the fruit begins to ripen keep a close eye on it, and cover it either with netting or with high cloches or the birds will have it first. When the grapes are thoroughly ripe they are pressed, yeast is added, and they are fermented in the usual way (see under "Grape Wine").

FROM CUTTINGS

If growing from cuttings, take your cuttings in the autumn. You need pieces of stem about 9 inches long, with a pair of buds at either end. Bury these a foot or so deep,

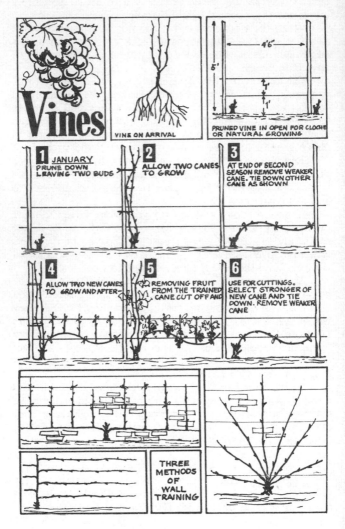

Vines

VINE ON ARRIVAL

PRUNED VINE IN OPEN FOR CLOCHE OR NATURAL GROWING

4'6"
5'
1'
1'

1 JANUARY PRUNE DOWN LEAVING TWO BUDS

2 ALLOW TWO CANES TO GROW

3 AT END OF SECOND SEASON REMOVE WEAKER CANE. TIE DOWN OTHER CANE AS SHOWN

4 ALLOW TWO NEW CANES TO GROW AND AFTER—

5 REMOVING FRUIT FROM THE TRAINED CANE CUT OFF AND

6 USE FOR CUTTINGS. SELECT STRONGER OF NEW CANE AND TIE DOWN. REMOVE WEAKER CANE

THREE METHODS OF WALL TRAINING

66

laying them horizontally, so that they will survive the winter, and in late March or early April dig them up, and set them just like any other cutting, with the topmost two buds at ground level. Sift some light soil in a little mound over the cutting (about $1\frac{1}{2}$ in. high will do) to prevent the wind from drying it out, or frost damage, mark the spot with a cane, and await results.

There are many ways of pruning, and training vines, and the illustration by George Hodgson shows some suggested ones.

Winemaking Circles

WINEMAKING as an "organised" hobby is a comparatively new thing, although wines have been made in these islands for centuries in the cottages of country folk. It was only in 1953 that the first "Winemakers' Circle" was formed at Andover, closely followed—quite independently and spontaneously—by others at Welwyn Garden City and Cheltenham.

In the last 20 years, however, the idea spread with astounding speed, and by now there are over 1,000 such clubs, scattered the length and breadth of the British Isles, and in Canada and the U.S.A., most of them following the original idea and calling themselves "Circles", some of them adopting the style of "Guilds", and yet others calling themselves "Societies" or "Associations". The publication of the monthly magazine, *The Amateur Winemaker*, from 1958 onwards has done much to consolidate the movement and publicise the aims of the Circles.

All of them have the same fundamental objective—the improvement of the standard of country wines—and all of them notably have the same characteristic, a striking friendliness and informality. The Circles are real centres of friendship and good fellowship, as well as means of instruction.

By buying apparatus and sometimes ingredients in bulk they are able to obtain discounts from many firms and thus can offer their members these goods at favourable rates.

Practical winemaking is learnt pleasantly and in a sociable atmosphere by means of talks, demonstrations, quizzes, and

67

competitions, and nowadays there are also inter-club contests. Members learn not only how to make wine, but how to exhibit and judge it.

On the social side, there are usually Christmas or New Year parties, dinners, dances, outings to breweries, sugar refineries, glassworks, potteries, wine lodges, vineyards, and other places of interest ot the winemaker.

All in all, members find that joining a Winemakers' Circle is definitely worth while, and anyone interested in the subject would be well advised to contact the nearest one, if they are lucky enough to have one in their area.

The first National Conference and Show—quite a small affair—was held at Andover in 1959, and others have followed at Bournemouth, Brighton, Harrow, Cheltenham, Clacton, Harrogate, Bognor and Torquay, and the "National" has now developed into a mammoth competitive wine show which can attract as many as 4,000 entries. It is allied to a week-end of lectures, discussions and merrymaking which is the big event of the year for keen winemakers, and visitors even come from abroad—Germany, Denmark and Canada, for instance.

The show has now grown into the National Association of Winemakers and Brewers (Amateur) and has also led to the formation in 1964 of The Amateur Winemakers' National Guild of Judges which set itself the task of getting down on paper a system of wine judging, notes for the guidance of show organisers, judges, and judges' stewards, and specimen schedules which clubs or organisations could adopt for their wine competitions.

A tremendous amount of ground work was done on this, and embodied in the handbook which the Guild eventually published, *Judging Home-made Wine* (25p) from *The Amateur Winemaker Publications Ltd.*, Andover. Also available is a most useful book by the Guild Chairman, S. W. Andrews, *Be A Wine Judge* (75p), postage 17p.

Winemaking spread outwards from Britain, and recent years have seen many wine circles on the British pattern being formed in America, Canada, Ireland, Rhodesia, Belgium, Holland, Australia and New Zealand. Obviously its appeal is· not confined to these islands!

Organising a wine competition

IF, as a winemaker, you wish to exhibit your wine competitively, you are not likely to encounter many difficulties, so long as you adhere rigidly to any conditions which are laid down in the show's schedule, and if your wine is up to standard, you may even win a prize! If, however, you are a club secretary or official, or even are known locally as someone who "knows a bit about wine", you are liable suddenly to find yourself faced with a request by some flower show or other to lay down rules and regulations for a wine class which the committee is thinking of including for the first time.

Your first action should be to study the Judges Guild handbook, *Judging Home-made Wines*, carefully.

Secondly, you have to decide how many, and what, classes you can have (or afford) on this occasion. You should bear in mind that a single wine class is not much use, for no judge can really judge a sweet wine side by side with a dry. Once he has tasted a really sweet wine his palate for drier wines is destroyed for that day! At least two classes are therefore desirable, and more if possible, and many Circles prefer grouping wines into Dry, Medium, and Sweet. It is not really possible to define these in terms of specific gravity; the best one can do is to say that a really dry wine is likely to be below 1000.

Given these three main classifications it is an age-old argument as to how wines should be further broken down into small numbers desirable for a class. Should they be described by ingredient, e.g., "Parsnip, sweet", "Red-currant, dry", or by purpose, e.g., Red table wine, dry", "Dessert wine, white"? There are two schools of thought, and the handbook caters for both by giving specimen schedules of all sizes in both systems. It is for you to decide which you prefer.

Having decided upon your classes, you can proceed to draw up some rules, and here are some of the points which you must obviously cover; others may well occur in individual cases.

RULES

Standard 26 oz. wine bottles and no half-bottles should

be used, and they should be of clear glass. (Even red wines should be shown in clear bottles, so that the colour can be judged.)

The airspace should be between $\frac{1}{4}$ in. and $\frac{3}{4}$ in.

No separate small tasting bottle (to avoid the necessity of opening the bottle exhibited) should be allowed, and exhibitors should be told that the actual bottle will be opened and tasted.

Bottles should be securely corked, preferably with a stopper cork, which may be wired for travelling.

Labels should preferably be supplied by the organisers, and be about 2 in. by $\frac{3}{4}$ in., so fixed that the bottom edge of the label is an inch above the bottom of the bottle. On the labels should appear only the description of the wine, by use or ingredient according to the type of schedule adopted.

Golden and tawny wines go in the white wine classes, rosé wines go with the reds if there are no separate classes.

Model rules are set out in the handbook.

Judging

HAVING covered all these points, turn your thoughts to the judges. What will they want? A good judge will bring his own kit—corkscrew, glasses, tea towel, marking sheet, etc., but it is of the greatest assistance if you can ensure that he is provided with glasses for tasting, a spittoon, water for washing up, and a vessel in which to do it, and a palate refresher—cheese, biscuits, bread, or something of that sort.

But how, I can hear you asking, does one actually *judge* wine? And here I run into difficulty, because it is just not possible to describe a taste with pen and paper. And that, of course, is the factor with which one is principally concerned. Taste, and knowledge of wine, is largely a matter of accumulated comparative experience, and it is up to every winemaker, whether he aspires to judge or not, steadily to increase his knowledge and experience of wine by comparing his own products with those of his fellow members and, indeed, with all types of commercial wine. Only in that way can he acquire the requisite experience, and it is one of the pleasantest aspects of our hobby, as you well know!

A National judge will assess the wine under these four main headings, for which he will award points as follows:

Presentation	2
Clarity and Colour	4
Bouquet	4
Flavour, Balance and Quality	20
	—
Total, out of	30

The first two factors he will assess before opening the bottle.

He will look at its general appearance (cleanliness, neatness and legibility of label, newness of cork, size of air space, etc.). The bottle should be well polished and, needless to say, scrupulously clean.

The judge will look through the neck of the bottle to judge the clarity of the wine, and at the conical "punt" at the bottom to judge its brilliance. Here there should not be the slightest trace of any yeast or other deposit. A star-bright wine will score points over a bright, or a merely clear, wine. A wise exhibitor bottles his wine for show several days ahead after having made sure that it has been adequately racked, and he thus minimises the risk of having any yeast deposit.

The bouquet must be enticing, making one want to taste the wine; it must be vinous, pleasing, and well developed, but not overpoweringly so.

But, when all is said and done, it is the taste of the wine which naturally carries the most marks. The flavour of a wine must be agreeable, reasonably redolent of the fruit or source of origin (though not so much as some expect), vinous and invigorating, with sufficient "bite", enough acid, adequate strength for its purpose (i.e., aperitif, table or dessert) and the correct degree of dryness or sweetness. It should, above all, be well balanced as between sweetness, acidity and astringency, and be free of bacterial or other faults.

Between tastes the judge will clear his palate with biscuit, bread, or something of that sort.

Judging procedure is set out in detail in *Be A Wine Judge* and wine clubs will find it fascinating to study these clear directions and arrange competitions to give their members judging practice. This can be done by having, say, up to 10 bottles of wine available and giving each member a judging sheet on which are set out the possible points to be scored under each heading.

To assist in a complete split-down of the marking, it helps if all the markings normally used by Guild judges are doubled (this, of course, does not affect the end result) and printed marking sheets so devised for practice judging are available from *The Amateur Winemaker*.

As long as members are using the same sheets, it is astonishing how similar are the verdicts obtained.

Recipes the year round

THE recipes are given under the months in which they are usually made, so that your winemaking can be practised all the year round, but they are also indexed alphabetically at the back of the book so that any one can be quickly found.

Since Britain has "gone metric", recipes are given in British, metric and U.S.A. measures, and readers may well find these conversion tables helpful.

WEIGHT

British to Metric

	5 lb.	=	2.267 kilogrammes
	4 lb.	=	1.814 kilos
	3 lb.	=	1.360 kilos
	2 lb.	=	907 grammes
	1 lb.	=	453 gms.
	½ lb.	=	226 gms.
	¼ lb.	=	113 gms.
	1 oz.	=	30 gms. (approx.)
Tablespoon	½ oz.	=	15 gms. (approx.)
Dessertspoon	¼ oz.	=	10 gms. (approx.)
Teaspoon	⅛ oz.	=	5 gms. (approx.)

Metric to British

5 kilogrammes	= 11 lb.
4 kilos	= 8 lb. 12 oz.
3 kilos	= 6 lb. 9 ozs.
2 kilos	= 4 lb. 6 ozs.
1 kilo	= 2 lb. 3 ozs.
500 grammes	= 1 lb. 1½ ozs.
250 gms.	= 8¾ ozs.
125 gms.	= 4½ ozs.
100 gms.	= 3½ ozs.
50 gms.	= 1½ ozs.

CAPACITY

British to Metric

	1 gallon	=	4.546 litres
		=	4546 millilitres (or c.c.s.)
	1 pint	=	568 ml/ccs.
	½ pint	=	284 ml/ccs.
	1 fl. oz.	=	28 ml/ccs.
Tablespoon	½ fl. oz.	=	15 ml/ccs. (approx.)
Dessertspoon	¼ fl. oz.	=	10 ml/ccs. (approx.)
Teaspoon	⅛ fl. oz.	=	5 ml/ccs. (approx.)

Metric to British

5 litres	= 8 pints 14 ozs.
4½ litres	= 7 pints 18 ozs.
4 litres	= 7 pints
3 litres	= 5 pints 5 ozs.
2 litres	= 3 pints 10 ozs.
1 litre	= 1 pint 14 ozs.
500 millilitres	= 17 ozs.
250 ml/ccs.	= 8½ ozs.
125 ml/ccs.	= 4¼ ozs.
100 ml/ccs.	= 3½ ozs.
50 ml/ccs.	= 1¾ ozs.

To convert	into	Multiply by
Pounds	Kilogrammes	.45359
Ounces	Grammes	28.3496
Grains	Grammes	.0648
Gallons	Litres	4.54596
Pints	Litres	.5683
Pints	Millilitres or Cubic centimetres	568.26
Fluid ounces	Millilitres or Cubic centimetres	28.413
Kilogrammes	Pounds	2.2046
Grammes	Ounces	.035274
Grammes	Grains	15.432
Litres	Gallons	.22
Litres	Pints	1.7598
To convert	into	Multiply by
Cubic centimetres or millilitres	Fluid ounces	.036
Fahrenheit	Centigrade	Subtract 32, multiply by 5, divide by 9.
Centigrade	Fahrenheit	Multiply by 9, divide by 5, and add 32.

American readers should note that the pound measure of weight as now used is the same in Britain, Canada, and U.S.A. (it equals roughly ½ kilo.) but the British and American gallons differ.

The Imperial or English gallon as used in Britain and Canada is of 8 pints, 160 liquid ozs., or 277¼ cubic inches, whereas the U.S.A. gallon is of 8 pints, 128 liquid ozs., or 231 cubic inches. (The American fluid ounce is slightly larger than the British, 16 U.S.A. ounces equalling 16½ British ounces). The English gallon thus equals 1.2 U.S.A. gallons. This accounts for the fact that in the recipes smaller quantities of ingredients are specified for use with the smaller U.S.A. gallon.

There are differences in spoon measures, too. The American teaspoon is only four-fifths the size of the British, but this difference can usually be ignored, since it is cancelled out by the fact that the gallon is also smaller. Two British tea-spoons equal one dessertspoon, and two dessertspoons one tablespoon, but the American "tablespoon" is the same size as the British "dessertspoon". This is allowed for in the recipes; all measures are in *level* and not "rounded" or heaped spoonsful.

In all the recipes use, preferably, a wine yeast, but failing that a level teaspoon of granulated yeast per gallon.

It is good practice to add 1 Campden tablet to each gallon of "must", and always to use a yeast nutrient.

If you are diabetic, and wish to make a safe wine always use the minimum sugar (2–2½ lb. per gallon, 250 gms. per litre) and a nutrient to ensure that you ferment it right out to dryness. The wine can be sweetened to taste when finished with Sorbitol.

Warning

Some plants and flowers are so poisonous that they must on no account be used for winemaking. Others are "doubtful" in that they may not be highly poisonous, particularly in the small quantities in which they might be employed in wine-making, but must still be highly suspect. The position is complicated by the fact that some substances used in wine-making, notably sugar and yeast, can sometimes neutralise poisons, so that occasionally safe wines may be made from apparently doubtful sources. But one cannot depend on this and we would urge winemakers NOT to use anything in the "poisonous" or "doubtful" categories. Our lists are by no means exhaustive and the only safe rule is: if in doubt about a material—don't use it.

Those "Not recommended" are so listed because, although we are often asked to supply recipes using them, they are not suitable winemaking material either because of fermentative difficulties or because they are not palatable.

POISONOUS: Aconite, alder, aquilegia, azalea, bane-berry, black nightshade, bluebell, buckthorn, buttercup, celandine, columbine, charlock, Christmas rose, clematis, cowbane, cuckoopint, cyclamen, daffodil, deadly nightshade,

January

delphinium, dwarf elder, fool's parsley, foxglove, most fungi, geranium, green potatoes, all hellebores, hemlock, henbane, holly, honeysuckle (the berries), horse-chestnut, laburnum, laurel, lilac, lilies-of-the-valley, lobelia, lupins, marsh marigolds, meadow rue, mezereon, mistletoe, monkswood, narcissus, pheasant's eye, peony, poppy, privet, rhododendron, rhubarb leaves, spearwort, spindleberry, sweet pea, thorn apple, traveller's joy, wood anemone, woody nightshade, yew.

DOUBTFUL: Borage, broom, carnation, chrysanthemum, clover, pinks.

NOT RECOMMENDED: Agrimony, cabbage, coconut, all fungi (including mushrooms), lettuce, marrow, potato, pumpkin, spinach, tomato, turnip.

JANUARY

BARLEY WINE

	British	Metric	U.S.A.
Barley	1 lb.	½ kilo	¾ lb.
Raisins	1 lb.	½ kilo	¾ lb.
or Grape			
Concentrate (white)	½ pint	280 mls.	½ pint
Potatoes	1 lb.	½ kilo	¾ lb.
Lemons	2	2	2
Sugar	3½ lb.	1½ kilos	2½ lb.
Campden tablet	1	1	1
Water	1 gallon	4½ litres	1 gallon
Yeast & nutrient			

Scrub (or peel if old) and chop the potatoes; grind the barley and raisins in a mincer, having soaked the grain in a pint of water overnight. Put sugar, barley, potatoes and raisins in a bowl and pour on hot (not necessarily boiling) water. Grape concentrate can be used instead of raisins.

Add the juice of the lemons. Allow to cool until tepid; add the crushed Campden tablet, yeast and nutrient. Leave it to stand in covered pan for 10 days, stirring well daily. Strain, put into fermenting vessel, and fit air-lock. Siphon off into bottles when clear and no longer fermenting. Ready after about six months.

FIG WINE

	British	Metric	U.S.A.
Brown sugar	2½ lb.	1 kilo	2 lb.
Dried figs	2 lb.	1 kilo	1½ lb.
Large raisins	½ lb.	¼ kilo	½ lb.
or Concentrate (white)	¼ pint	140 mls.	¼ pint
Lemon	1	1	1
Orange	1	1	1
Root ginger (optional)	½ oz.	15 gms.	½ oz.
Boiling water	1 gallon	4½ litres	1 gallon
Yeast & nutrient			

Chop the figs and raisins and place in a large crock with the sugar, the grated lemon and orange rinds (no white pith) and the juice of the two fruits, a cupful of grape concentrate can be used instead of the raisins. Bruise the ginger and add that. Bring the water to the boil, and pour it over the ingredients, stirring well to dissolve the sugar, and adding one crushed Campden tablet. When the liquor has cooled to about 70°F., cool enough for you to be able to put your finger in it comfortably, stir in the yeast, cover the crock closely, and leave it in a warm place (about 70°F., 21°C.) for 12 days, stirring daily. After that strain into fermenting jar or bottle and fit air-lock, and move into a temperature of about 65°F. (17°C.). After another two months the ferment will probably have finished; when the wine has cleared, siphon it off into clean bottles. It is best kept at least a year from the date of making but can well be sampled within six months—and no doubt will be!

MAIZE WINE

	British	Metric	U.S.A.
Crushed maize	1½ lb.	¾ kilo	1 lb.
Demerara sugar	3½ lb.	1½ kilos	3 lb.
Sweet oranges	4	4	4
Lemon	1	1	1
Raisins	1 lb.	½ kilo	¾ lb.
or Concentrate (white)	½ pint	280 mls.	½ pint
Water	1 gallon	4½ litres	1 gallon
Yeast & nutrient			

Despite the amount of sugar, this will make a medium wine, and there are many similar recipes which advocate up

January

to as much as even 4½ lb. sugar, so if you prefer a sweet wine you can well exceed the normal 3½ lb. limit in this case. It is a help to soak the maize overnight in some of the water to soften it, and then, when you come to make your wine, run it through a coarse mincer, together with the raisins. A cupful of grape concentrate can be substituted for the raisins. Peel the lemon and oranges, being careful to miss the white pith, and put the rinds into a crock with the sugar, maize, raisins, and the juice of the fruits. Pour over the ingredients the water, which need be only hot (not boiling) add one crushed Campden tablet, and stir well to dissolve it and the sugar. Allow the liquor to cool to 70°F. (21°C), then add the yeast and yeast nutrient and keep the crock in a warm place, closely covered, for 10 days, stirring well each day. Then strain into fermenting jar or bottle and fit air-lock.

PRUNE WINE

	British	Metric	U.S.A.
Prunes	2 lb.	1 kilo	1¾ lb.
Raisins	½ lb.	¼ kilo	¼ lb.
or Concentrate (white)	¼ pint	140 mls.	¼ pint
Sugar	3½ lb.	1½ kilos	3 lb.
Campden tablet	1	1	1
Water	1 gallon	4½ litres	1 gallon
Yeast & nutrient; pectic enzyme			

Put the prunes in a crock with the water and enzyme, mashing and stirring them daily for 10 days. Then strain, and either press the pulp or squeeze it by hand to extract as much juice and flavour as possible. Add the sugar, chopped raisins or grape concentrate, and a crushed Campden tablet, and stir to dissolve. Then add the yeast and yeast nutrient and leave to ferment in a warm place, as usual, for 10 days. Keep the crock lcosely covered and stir daily. Then strain into fermenting jar and fit air-lock, and move into slightly cooler place (about 65°F., 17°C.). After another two months the secondary ferment should be finished and when the wine clears it should be racked off into clean bottles.

78

RAISIN WINE

	British	Metric	U.S.A.
Large raisins	8 lb.	3½ kilos	6½ lb.
Citric acid	1 tablesp.	1 tablesp.	2 tablesp.
Campden tablet	1	1	1
Water	1 gallon	4½ litres	1 gallon
Yeast & nutrient			

Clean the raisins thoroughly by washing them in a colander, then mince through a coarse mincer. Put them into a fermentation jar with a wide neck, pour on the cold water, and add one crushed Campden tablet. Keep the jar covered. Two days later add the yeast, acid, and nutrient, and fit air-lock to the jar. Alternatively cover the wide neck with a sheet of polythene secured by a rubber band, which will serve the same purpose. Keep the fermentation jar in a warm place (about 70°F., 21°C.) for a few days, and afterwards in a temperature of about 65°F. (17°C.) until the ferment has finished. Each day give the vessel a good shake. When fermentation has finished strain the liquor off the raisins, which can then easily be removed (hence the need for a wide-necked jar, with a narrow-necked one it can be a fiddly business). Put into a fresh jar and leave for a further three months before racking (siphoning the wine off the lees) again and bottling.

By using some sugar one can reduce the amount of raisins required, although the wine will have nothing like the same body. Here is a recipe, however, using this method:

RAISIN WINE (2)

	British	Metric	U.S.A.
Large raisins	2 lb.	1 kilo	1½ lb.
Sugar	2 lb.	1 kilo	1¾ lb.
Water	1 gallon	4½ litres	1 gallon
Citric acid	1 teasp.	1 teasp.	1 teasp.
Yeast & nutrient			

Mince the raisins, put them in the water, and boil for an hour. Strain the liquor on to the sugar, stir well to dissolve, allow to cool to 70°F. (21°C.) and pour into fermenting bottle. Add the yeast, acid and nutrient. Keep in a warm place until it begins to clear, then rack for the first time, into a clean jar,

January

re-fitting air-lock. When the fermentation ceases completely siphon into clean bottles and cork.

GRAPEFRUIT WINE

	British	Metric	U.S.A.
Large grapefruit	6	6	6
Sugar	3½ lb.	1½ kilos	3 lb.
Water	1 gallon	4½ litres	1 gallon
Yeast & nutrient			

Clean the fruit and grate the skins finely. Put the water, gratings and juice into a bowl, and add the yeast. Stand the bowl in a warm place (70°F., 21°C. is ideal), covered closely, and leave for five or six days, stirring thoroughly twice daily. Strain off the liquor through a nylon sieve, or two or three thicknesses of muslin, and dissolve the sugar in it. Put into fermenting jar and fit air-lock. Leave to ferment out, and when this has happened rack into clean bottles and cork firmly.

CITRUS WINE

	British	Metric	U.S.A.
Raisins	1 lb.	½ kilo	¾ lb.
or Concentrate (white)	½ pint	280 mls.	½ pint
Grapefruit	3	3	3
Lemons	3	3	3
Oranges	3	3	3
Sugar	3½ lb.	1½ kilos	3 lb.
Water	1 gallon	4½ litres	1 gallon

Firstly peel the fruit (do not squeeze the skins or include any white pith) keeping the peel as intact as possible so it can be retrieved easily later. Put water into a crock and add the chopped-up fruit and sugar, stirring thoroughly to dissolve the latter. Then add the yeast and yeast nutrient, cover closely, and leave in a warm place (about 70°F., 21°C.) for a fortnight, stirring daily. At the end of this period take out the peel and, having strained off the liquor, squeeze out the fruit pulp and add the resultant juice to the bulk. Put into fermenting jar and fit air-lock, and leave to ferment out. Siphon it into clean bottles when it has done so.

January

DATE WINE

	British	Metric	U.S.A.
Dates	3 lb.	1½ kilos	2¼ lb.
Sugar	2 lb.	1 kilo	1½ lb.
Citric acid	1 tablesp.	1 tablesp.	2 tablesps.
Grape tannin	1 teasp.	1 teasp.	1 teasp.
Water	1 gallon	4½ litres	1 gallon
Yeast & nutrient; pectic enzyme			

What better use for dates left over from Christmas! Chop or mince the dates and pour over them the boiling water, in which the sugar has been dissolved. Cover the pan closely with a heavy cloth and add the other ingredients when cool. Ferment on the "pulp" for a week and then strain into fermenting jar and fit air-lock, topping up with a little cold water if necessary. Ferment out, rack when clear, and bottle.

"INSTANT WINE"
by A. S. Henderson

If you have just started winemaking and want an 8% wine which is suitable for table use, quickly made, rapid to mature, and low-priced, try this "instant wine" recipe:

	British	Metric	U.S.A.
Tinned grapefruit juice	1 pint	½ litre	1 pint
Light dried malt (Edme)	½ lb.	¼ kilo	½ lb.
Sugar	1 lb.	½ kilo	¾ lb.
Water	1 gallon	4½ litres	1 gallon
Yeast & nutrient			

Dissolve the sugar in up to ½ gallon of water, putting the saucepan over a very low heat to speed up the solution. Meanwhile dissolve the dried malt extract in a little cold water, open the tin of fruit juice, and funnel everything into the fermentation jar. Dissolve the yeast nutrient with a little warm water and add to the jar, top up with cold water to the shoulder (this should reduce the whole to a safe temperature) and add the yeast. Shake well, and fit an air-lock. Stand in a warm place and watch it go! Within 24 hours the stream of bubbles should be continuous, not less than one per second.

81

February

After a day or two, a thick layer will form on the bottom. Give the jar a swirl round daily to agitate the deposit. When gravity has dropped to 1004, or less (10–14 days), filter. Boil a little filter pulp for 2 mins. in half a pint of water, place a piece of clean linen in a funnel and pour the filter pulp on to it, then pour the wine carefully on to the "pulp" so as not to disturb it. Return the first few wine glassfuls to the funnel until the filtrate looks reasonably clear. Repeat the filtration two or three days later, and keep the finished wine a week in a cool place before drinking. Other fruit juices (except, God forbid, tomato!) can be used in the same way.

FEBRUARY
TINNED PEACH, APRICOT, OR NECTARINE

	British	Metric	U.S.A.
Tinned peach slices	15½ ozs.	½ kilo	19 fl. ozs.
Sugar	1½ lb.	675 gms.	1 lb.
Malt extract	½ lb.	¼ kilo	½ lb.
Citric acid	1 teasp.	1 teasp.	1 teasp.
Tannin	½ teasp.	½ teasp.	½ teasp.
Water	1 gallon	4½ litres	1 gallon

Sauternes yeast & nutrient; pectic enzyme

The peaches can be bought in slices in either 15½ oz. or 16 oz. tins, as halves in 16 oz. tins, or labelled "white peaches" in 16 oz. tins. Wine firms also sell peach pulp. One 15½ oz. or 16 oz. tin of either will make, using the quantities in the recipe, a light dry table wine, but if a fuller-bodied wine is required use two tins of peaches (roughly 2 lb.)—they are quite cheap—and increase the sugar to 2¾ lb. (U.S.A. 2¼ lb.) the citric acid to 2 teaspoons, and the tannin to 1 teaspoon.

Pour any syrup into your fermenting jar, then mash the fruit with a stainless steel spoon. Boil two quarts of water and dissolve the sugar and malt extract in it, then put "pulp" into polythene bucket and pour the boiling syrup over it. Allow to cool to tepid (70°F., 21°C.) before adding acid, tannin and pectic enzyme. Stir well, cover closely, and leave in a warm place. Next day stir, pour the whole into the fermenting jar with the syrup from the can, and add yeast,

February

nutrient, and enough cold water to bring level of "must" to just below the shoulder of the jar, leaving room for a "head". Fir air-lock and leave in a warm place for 10 days, shaking jar daily to disperse pulp through liquid. Then strain into fresh jar, and top up to bottom of neck with water. Ferment out, racking and bottling as usual. For a sweet wine use 1 lb. 12 oz. tin of pulp and 3¼ lb. of sugar.

ALMOND WINE

	British	Metric	U.S.A.
Raisins	1 lb.	½ kilo	1 lb.
or Concentrate (white)	½ pint	280 mls.	½ pint
Almonds	1½ ozs.	50 gms.	1½ ozs.
Sugar	2 lb.	1½ kilos	2¼ lb.
Lemons	2	2	2
Water	1 gallon	4½ litres	1 gallon
Yeast & nutrient			

The almonds and raisins should be minced and then boiled gently in the water for about an hour. If you prefer, grape concentrate can be substituted for the raisins, and added at the end of the boiling. Add enough fresh water to make the quantity up to one gallon again. Strain the liquor on to the sugar, stirring well to dissolve, then add the juice and grated rind of the lemons, taking care to include no white pith. Add the yeast and nutrient, when the temperature has dropped to 70°F. (21°C.), and endeavour to maintain roughly that temperature for 10 days, keeping the crock closely covered. Then strain the wine through a nylon sieve into the fermenting bottle and fit air-lock. Leave until it begins to clear and then rack.

DRIED BILBERRY WINE
(or Elderberry or Sloe)

	British	Metric	U.S.A.
Dried bilberries	½ lb.	¼ kilo	¼ lb.
Raisins	¼ lb.	100 gms.	¼ lb.
or Concentrate (red)	¼ pint	100 mls.	¼ pint
Sugar	2½ lb.	1¼ kilos	2 lb.
Citric acid	1 teasp.	1 teasp.	1 teasp.
Water	1 gallon	4½ litres	1 gallon
Yeast & nutrient; pectic enzyme			

February

Put the chopped raisins or the grape concentrate in the boiling water, with the bilberries and the sugar. Stir well to dissolve sugar. Allow to cool, add acid, enzyme, nutrient and yeast. Keep covered in a warm place and stir daily for a week, pushing the fruit down. Strain into fermenting jar, ferment, rack when clear, and bottle. An excellent dry red table wine, best made with a Bordeaux or Pommard yeast. For a sweet wine increase sugar to 3 lb. and use a Burgundy yeast.

N.B.—It is possible to take a second "run" off the discarded fruit by adding another gallon of boiling water, more sugar, more nutrient and more acid. When it cools, add some of the first batch of fermenting wine as a starter and ferment for 10 days on the pulp, and continue as before. A lighter wine will result.

MANGOLD WINE

	British	Metric	U.S.A.
Mangolds	5 lb.	2¼ kilos	3¾ lb.
Sugar	3 lb.	1½ kilos	2¼ lb.
Lemons	2	2	2
Oranges	2	2	2
Water	1 gallon	4½ litres	1 gallon
Yeast & nutrient			

Wash the mangolds but do not peel. Cut into pieces and boil until tender. Strain, and to every gallon of liquor add sugar and rinds of oranges and lemons (avoid the white pith) as above, and boil for 20 minutes. Allow the liquor to cool, and add the juice of the oranges and lemons. Stir in the yeast (a general purpose wine yeast or a level teaspoonful of granulated yeast) and leave in a warm place, well covered, for about a week. Then stir, transfer to fermenting bottle or jar, and air-lock. When the wine clears, rack it off with a siphon into a clean storage vessel. Keep it for another six months in a cool place, then bottle.

February

ORANGE OR TANGERINE WINE

	British	Metric	U.S.A.
Sweet oranges	12	12	12
Sugar	3½ lb.	1½ kilos	2¾ lb.
Water	1 gallon	4½ litres	1 gallon
Yeast & nutrient			

Peel six of the oranges thinly, avoiding the white pith like the plague (it imparts a most bitter taste to the wine). Pour a quart of boiling water on to the rind and allow to stand for 24 hours, then strain off the water into a bowl containing three quarts of water and the sugar. Cut all the oranges in half and squeeze the juice into the bowl. Stir until the sugar is dissolved, and then add the yeast. If you use a general purpose wine yeast, which is to be recommended, the liquor can safely be strained from the crock into a fermenting jar, and fitted with air-lock, within two or three days. Siphon it off the lees for the first time when it clears, and re-bottle two or three months later.

SEVILLE ORANGE WINE

	British	Metric	U.S.A.
Thin-skinned Seville oranges	24	24	20
Lemons	4	4	3
Sugar	8 lb.	4 kilos	6 lb.
Water	2 gallons	9 litres	2 gallons
Yeast & nutrient; pectic enzyme			

Peel 12 of the oranges and throw away the peel. Cut up oranges and lemons into slices and put in earthenware pan. Boil the water and pour on, boiling. Place in moderately warm corner and when tepid add yeast, enzyme and wine yeast or a teaspoonful of granulated yeast; stir each day for a fortnight. Strain, then add sugar and stir until dissolved. Put in a 2-gallon jar, filling up to top. Put surplus in black bottles (bottles must be dark or wine will lose its colour). Use this for filling up large jar. Ferment to completion under air-lock, rack when it clears, and bottle two months later.

February

COFFEE WINE

	British	Metric	U.S.A.
Instant coffee (Nescafé)	1 level tablesp.	15 gms.	2 tablesps.
Sugar	2½ lb.	1¼ kilos	2 lb.
Citric acid	1 tablesp.	15 gms.	2 tablesps.
Water	1 gallon	4½ litres	1 gallon
Ammonium phosphate	1 teasp.	1 teasp.	1 teasp.

Put coffee, sugar, citric acid and ammonium phosphate in mixing bowl and pour on 4 pints (2 litres) of boiling water. Stir well. Allow to cool, pour into fermenting jar, top up with warm water to shoulder, introduce yeast. Fit air-lock. After five days top up with water to bottom of neck, refit air-lock, ferment out, rack and bottle as usual.

PARSNIP SHERRY (Oloroso)

	British	Metric	U.S.A.
Parsnips	4½ lb.	2 kilos	4½ lb.
Hops	½ oz.	20 gms.	½ oz.
Malt extract	½ lb.	¼ kilo	½ lb.
Brown sugar	4 lb.	2 kilo	3 lb.
Gravy browning (liquid)	1 teasp.	1 teasp.	1 teasp.
Lemons	2	2	2
Water	1 gallon	4½ litres	1 gallon
Yeast & nutrient			

Clean parsnips, but do not peel, and ensure that their weight is not less than four pounds after cleaning. Cut them into slices and boil gently in half the water until soft (but not mushy, or the wine will not clear). Then strain into a pan. Put the hops in a bag in the remaining water and boil gently for half an hour, then stir in the gravy browning (which is only caramel colouring). Mix the liquids together and stir in the malt and sugar, allow to cool to blood heat, and then add yeast. Keep warm and closely covered and ferment for 14 days, then stir, siphon into fermenting jar and fit air-lock.

March

When the wine clears siphon off into sterilised bottles and keep for a further six months.

BANANA WINE

	British	Metric	U.S.A.
Peeled bananas	4 lb.	2 kilos	3 lb.
Banana skins	½ lb.	¼ kilo	½ lb.
Raisins	¼ lb.	¼ kilo	½ lb.
or Concentrate (white)	¼ lb.	100 mls.	¼ lb.
Lemon	1	1	1
Orange	1	1	1
Sugar	3 lb.	1½ kilos	2¼ lb.
Water	1 gallon	4½ litres	1 gallon
Yeast & nutrient			

Use black or spotted bananas, whatever you can scrounge. Place bananas and fruit peel into a cloth bag and put the bag, tied up, into a large saucepan or boiler with the water. Bring to the boil, then gently simmer for half an hour. Pour the hot liquor over the sugar and fruit juice, and when the cloth bag has cooled squeeze it with the hands to extract as much liquor as possible. When all the liquor is lukewarm (70°F., 21°C.) add the yeast. Leave it in a warm place for a week, stirring daily, then pour into a glass jar and move to a cooler place; it will be a thick-looking mess, like a lot of soapsuds. Keep it well covered and in a couple of months it will have a large sediment at the bottom. Siphon off, then add the chopped raisins or grape concentrate. Fit an air-lock and siphon off again after four months; by then it will have started to clear. Leave a further six months before sampling. It improves the longer you keep it.

BIRCH SAP WINE

This is a wine which, intriguing by its novelty, is also an excellent wine in its own right. It is probably of Baltic origin and during the last century was a popular drink in Russia, so much so that upon occasions whole forests of young birch trees were killed by the peasantry, who tapped them too enthusiastically . . . so beware of that error. No harm

March

will come to a tree by the loss of a gallon or so of sap in the spring (about the first fortnight in March) but the hole must afterwards be plugged with a wooden plug, and can then be used again next year. I am also told, although I can produce no written authority for it, that birch sap wine was a favourite with the Prince Consort, who doubtless had plenty of trees at his disposal!

The main precautions to observe are that you do not tap a very young tree—it should be at least 9 in. diameter—that you bore only far enough into the tree for your tap or tube to be held securely (bore to just beyond the inside of the bark where the sap rises and not into the "dead wood" of the centre of the trunk), that you do not take more than a gallon of sap from one tree, and that you plug the hole afterwards. Neglect of any of these points may harm the tree.

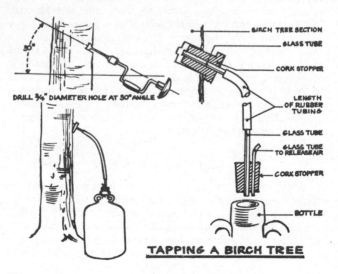

DRILL ¾" DIAMETER HOLE AT 30° ANGLE

BIRCH TREE SECTION
GLASS TUBE
CORK STOPPER
LENGTH OF RUBBER TUBING
GLASS TUBE
GLASS TUBE TO RELEASE AIR
CORK STOPPER
BOTTLE

TAPPING A BIRCH TREE

March

	British	Metric	U.S.A.
Birch sap	1 gallon	4½ litres	1 gallon
Lemons	2	2	2
Sweet oranges	1	1	1
Raisins	1 lb.	½ kilo	¾ lb.
or Concentrate (white)	½ pint	280 mls.	½ pint
Sugar	3 lb.	1½ kilos	2¼ lb.
Seville orange	1	1	1
Yeast & nutrient			

Obtain a wooden beer or wine-barrel tap, a piece of glass or plastic tubing, or even a piece of bamboo cane with the pith removed. With a brace and bit of the same diameter as tap or tube bore a hole into the trunk of the tree to just beyond the inside of the bark, and insert the tube, which should incline slightly downwards to allow the sap to run easily. In March, when the sap is rising, it should be possible to draw off a gallon or so of liquor in two or three days. Plug the hole afterwards.

Peel the oranges and lemons (discard all white pith) and boil the peel in the sap for 20 minutes. Add enough water to restore the volume of one gallon, then pour into a crock containing the sugar and chopped raisins. Stir until sugar is dissolved; when the liquor has cooled to 70°F. (21°C.) add the fruit juice and yeast. Cover the crock with a thick cloth and keep in a warm place until fermentation has quietened. Then strain into fermenting jar and fit air-lock. Leave for about six months, then siphon off and bottle. Use strong bottles, tie down the corks, and store the bottles on their sides for at least another six months before sampling.

Sycamore and walnut sap wines can be made in the same manner and an excellent beer can be produced by reducing the sugar to 1 lb.

PINEAPPLE WINE

	British	Metric	U.S.A.
Pineapples	4	4	4
Sugar	3¼ lb.	1¾ kilos	2¾ lb.
Lemons	2	2	2
Water	1 gallon	4½ litres	1 gallon
Yeast & nutrient			

March

"Top and bottom" the pineapples, then slice them into a 1-gallon saucepan and cover with a third of water. Bring to boil, and simmer for 25 minutes. Strain on to sugar in earthenware crock, and add remaining two-thirds of water, cold. Add the juice of the lemons. Stir well to dissolve sugar thoroughly, and leave to cool to blood heat. Then add yeast (wine yeast, a level teaspoonful of dried yeast, or ¾ oz. of baker's yeast), and a yeast nutrient if desired. (I used a general purpose wine yeast and a teaspoonful of a proprietary nutrient). Cover the pan closely for a week and leave it in a warm place, giving a daily stir, and then transfer to fermenting jars or bottles, which should be filled to the bottom of the neck and fitted with air-locks. Keep in temperature of about 60°F. (15°C.) until the wine begins to clear and has thrown a substantial sediment, then siphon off into clean bottles. Allow it to throw a fresh sediment, then siphon off into clean bottles and cork. This is a delicious light wine with a delightful bouquet.

PINEAPPLE LIQUEUR

Buy a big juicy pineapple and try your hand at making this really delightful liqueur. Slice the pineapple thinly, sprinkle with a little sugar, and leave for 24 hours. Press out the juice, measure it, and add an equal amount of brandy to which sugar has been added in the proportion of 2 ozs. sugar to every half pint of brandy. Put in a jar with a few slices of fresh pineapple and leave for three weeks, then strain and bottle.

RICE AND RAISIN

	British	Metric	U.S.A.
Raisins	3 lb.	1½ kilos	2¼ lb.
Rice	5 lb.	2¼ kilos	3¾ lb.
Sugar	10 lb.	4½ kilos	7½ lb.
Yeast	2 ozs.	50 gms.	2 ozs.
Water	3 gallons	13½ litres	3 gallons
Juice of 2 oranges and 2 lemons			

Dissolve sugar in some heated water taken from the 3

gallons. Allow to cool and pour over rice and raisins (do not chop or mince the raisins). Then add the juice, remaining water and sprinkle on yeast. Stir and leave in a warm place. Stir daily for 21 days then strain through muslin into three 1-gallon jars. Fit air-locks to the jars and keep them in a warm place until fermentation stops. Strain through a fine piece of muslin or filter paper. Then filter the wine through one of the popular filters and it is then ready for drinking straight away. If it is not drunk within 2 months add 1 Campden tablet per gallon and leave for 9 months.

Do not discard the pulp as it can be used to make a lighter wine. Dissolve 8 lb. of sugar in a gallon of hot water and pour on to the rice and raisin residue. Add 1½ gallons of cold water plus the juice from 2 oranges and 2 lemons together with 1 oz. of Allinsons dried yeast. Follow the same procedure as given for the first batch.

DRIED PEACH WINE

	British	Metric	U.S.A.
Dried peaches	2 lb.	1 kilo	2 lb.
Sugar	3½ lb.	1½ kilos	2¼ lb.
Citric acid	1 dessertsp.	2 teasps.	1 tablesp.
Water	1 gallon	4½ litres	1 gallon
Yeast & nutrient; pectic enzyme			

Soak the peaches for 12 hours in the cold water, then place all in a large saucepan or preserving pan, bring to the boil, and simmer for five or six minutes. Strain the liquid off into a crock, add the sugar, yeast nutrient, and enzyme and stir well until all is dissolved. Allow to cool to about 70°F. (21°C.), then add the acid and a general-purpose wine yeast starter or a level teaspoonful of granulated yeast. Cover the bowl closely and keep it in a temperature of 70–75°F. (21–24°C.) for four days, giving it a daily stir; then stir, transfer to fermenting jar, and fit air-lock. When wine clears and fermentation has finished, siphon it off the sediment into clean bottles and cork securely.

April

VIN ORDINAIRE

WHITE

	British	Metric	U.S.A.
Canned orange juice	½ pint	¼ litre	10 ozs.
Canned pine-apple juice	½ pint	¼ litre	10 ozs.
Sugar	2 lb.	1 kilo	1½ lb.
Water	1 gallon	4½ litres	1 gallon
Bordeaux yeast; pectic enzyme			

The sugar is poured into a gallon jar, the juices and nutrients, etc., are added and the jar is topped up to the shoulder with cold water. Vigorous stirring will dissolve the sugar and the yeast starter and Pectolase are added immediately. This wine will ferment out to dryness in about 3–4 weeks at 75°F. (21°C.). At the end of this time 2 Campden tablets should be added and the wine racked a week later. After 3–4 months the wine is brilliantly clear and is drinkable as a rough white wine but is much improved if cask matured for two months.

RED

	British	Metric	U.S.A.
Fresh elderberries	1 lb.	½ kilo	1 lb.
(or dried)	¼ lb.	100 gms.	¼ lb.
Raisins	1 lb.	½ kilo	1 lb.
or Concentrate (red)	½ pint	280 mls.	½ pint
Sugar	1½ lb.	¾ kilo	1½ lb.
Citric acid	1 dessertsp.	2 teasps.	1 tablesp.
Water	1 gallon	4½ litres	1 gallon
Burgundy yeast & nutrient; pectic enzyme			

The ingredients are crushed and placed in a bucket and boiling water is poured over them. The water level is brought up to 1 gallon and when cool the yeast starter and Pectolase are added. The "pulp" is strained off after four days and thereafter the fermentation continues in a gallon jar. Rack when all sugar has been used up (generally within a month) and allow to clear.

LEMON OR LIME WINES

	British	Metric	U.S.A.
Lemons or limes	10–12 (according to size)	10–12	10
Sugar	3 lb.	1½ kilos	2½ lb.
Raisins	2 lb.	1 kilo	1½ lb.
or Concentrate (white)	1 pint	560 mls.	1 pint
Water	1 gallon	4½ litres	1 gallon

Burgundy yeast & nutrient; pectic enzyme

Grate the peel from the fruit, but avoid getting any white pith, and pour it over the minced raisins or concentrate and the sugar, the water, boiling. When cool, add the juice of the lemons or limes, the yeast nutrient and a general purpose wine yeast, cover closely and ferment on the "pulp" for about a week. Then strain into fermenting jar, fit air-lock, and continue as usual.

BEES WINE

"You used to stand it in the window, and the bees used to go up and down in the liquid . . . it made quite a pleasant drink." When you hear someone saying this they are quite certainly talking about that old novelty, "Bees Wine", otherwise known as Palestinian or Californian Bees or Balm of Gilead. Actually the "bees" are merely a certain type of yeast (or rather a mixture of yeasts and bacteria) which has clumping properties—hence its name, *Saccharomyces Pryiformis*.

As the clumps of yeast form the carbon dioxide which is given off during fermentation carries them to the surface, where the bubbles disperse and allow the clumps to sink to the bottom again. The yeast clumps do thus move up and down and are rather like "busy little bees". Presumably "standing the jar on the windowsill" allowed it to get some sunshine, and therefore warmth to speed the fermentation, as well as light to show off the movement of the "bees".

Nowadays it is quite difficult to obtain a culture, the only source of which we know being the Brewing Industry Research Foundation at Nutfield, Surrey, though other yeast laboratories might be able to help.

To make Bees Wine, dissolve about 2 ozs. of brown sugar in one pint of cold water in a cylindrical, wide mouthed jar—

April

a Kilner jar or vase will do—pop in your "Bees". Add a pinch of citric acid, and a little yeast nutrient and cover the jar with a handkerchief. Each day for a week add 1 teaspoon of sugar and 1 teaspoon of ground ginger. Then dissolve 3½ teacups of sugar in 4 teacups of boiling water, and make up to five pints with cold water. Add a teaspoon of citric acid, and strain the liquid from the "bees" into the syrup, stirring the bulk well as you do so. Bottle your Bees Wine in screw-stoppered bottles but leave the stoppers loose for three hours, then screw down. The Bees Wine should be ready to drink in a fortnight. The "bees" themselves will have doubled in quantity, so they can be halved, and each portion used to start a new batch.

PRIMROSE WINE

	British	Metric	U.S.A.
Primroses	1 gallon	4½ litres	1 gallon
Sugar	3½ lb.	1½ kilos	2¾ lb.
Oranges	2	2	2
Lemon	1	1	1
Grape tannin	1 teasp.	1 teasp.	1 teasp.
Water	1 gallon	4½ litres	1 gallon
Yeast & nutrient			

Bring the water to the boil and stir into it the sugar, making sure that it is all dissolved. Put the peel of the oranges and lemon into a crock, bowl or polythene bucket, being careful to exclude all white pith, to prevent the wine from having a bitter taste, and pour the hot syrup over the rinds. Allow to cool to 70°F. (21°C.), then add the flowers, the fruit juice, tannin, your chosen yeast, and some yeast nutrient. Cover closely and leave for five days in a warm place, stirring each day. Then strain through a nylon sieve or muslin into a fermenting jar, filling it to the bottom of the neck, and fit an air-lock. Leave for three months, then siphon the wine off the yeast deposit into a fresh jar. A further racking after another three months is helpful, and shortly after that the wine will be fit to drink, if still young.

Later in the month, and right up till July, you can make another flower wine which is thought by many to be one of the most agreeable table wines, when made reasonably dry, gorse.

GORSE WINE

	British	Metric	U.S.A.
Gorse flowers	1 gallon	4½ litres	1 gallon
Sugar	3 lb.	1½ kilos	2½ lb.
Oranges	2	2	2
Lemons	2	2	2
Grape tannin	1 teasp.	1 teasp.	1 teasp.
Water	1 gallon	4½ litres	1 gallon
Yeast & nutrient			

The best plan is to put your flowers in a calico bag, which can then be dropped into the water and simmered for a quarter of an hour, afterwards making up the water to the original quantity. When you remove the bag, squeeze it well to extract the liquor, and return this to the bulk. Then dissolve the sugar in the liquid, and add the lemon and orange juice, and the skins (no pith) of the fruit. Allow the liquor to cool to 70°F. (21°C), then add the tannin, general-purpose wine yeast, or a level teaspoon of granulated yeast, and yeast nutrient. Three days is sufficient for fermentation to get well under way, as long as the liquor is kept in a warm place (65–70°F., 17–21°C.), closely covered and given an occasional stir. Then strain it into a fermenting jar and fit an air-lock and put in a slightly cooler place. Siphon it off the lees when the top third has cleared (after two or three months) and again three months later. Put in a cooler place still (55°F., 13°C.); it will be ready to drink after another two months or so.

COLTSFOOT WINE

Colstfoot grows abundantly in the British Isles but the flowers are not always easy to come by in quantity unless you have previously earmarked the plant's position. It is usually to be found in waysides, railway embankments and waste places, the bright yellow flowers putting in an appearance from March onwards, long in advance of the heart-shaped leaves. Because of this the old country name for this plant was "Son Before Father!" (Those who do not live in the country can obtain the dried flowers from a herbalist. One small packet will make a gallon.)

April

	British	Metric	U.S.A.
Coltsfoot flowers	1 gallon	4½ litres	1 gallon
Sugar	3½ lb.	1½ kilos	2¾ lb.
Oranges	2	2	2
Lemons	2	2	2
Grape tannin	1 teasp.	1 teasp.	1 teasp.
Water	1 gallon	4½ litres	1 gallon
Yeast & nutrient			

Dissolve the sugar in the water and bring to the boil. Simmer for five minutes. Remove from the heat and allow to cool. Peel the oranges and lemons thinly, and put the rinds into a bowl or stone jar with the juice, tannin and the flowers (just the heads). Pour over the cold syrup, and stir. Add the yeast mixed with a little of the lukewarm liquid and leave to ferment for seven days in a warm place, well covered. Stir daily. Strain into a fermenting jar, cover, or insert an air-lock. When fermentation ceases, siphon off and bottle.

COWSLIP WINE

	British	Metric	U.S.A.
Cowslip flowers	1 gallon	4½ litres	1 gallon
Sugar	3½ lb.	1½ kilos	2¾ lb.
Oranges	2	2	2
Lemon	1	1	1
Grape tannin	1 teasp.	1 teasp.	1 teasp.
Water	1 gallon	4½ litres	1 gallon
Yeast & nutrient			

Do not use the green stalks and lower parts of the flowers, but only the yellow portions. This is rather fiddling, but does protect the taste and colour. (*Method: As Coltsfoot.*)

DANDELION WINE (1)

	British	Metric	U.S.A.
Dandelions	3 quarts	3 litres	3 quarts
Sugar	3 lb.	1½ kilos	2¼ lb.
Lemons	2	2	2
Orange	1	1	1
Raisins	1 lb.	½ kilo	¾ lb.
or Concentrate (white)	½ pint	280 mls.	½ pint
Grape tannin	1 teasp.	1 teasp.	1 teasp.
Water	1 gallon	4½ litres	1 gallon
Yeast & nutrient			

April

The flowers must be freshly gathered (traditionally St. George's Day, April 23rd, is the correct occasion), picked off their stalks, and put into a large bowl. One does not need to pick off the petals: use the whole heads. Bring the water to the boil, pour over the dandelions, and leave for two days, stirring each day. Keep the bowl closely covered. On the third day, turn all into a boiler, add the sugar and the rinds only of the lemons and orange. Boil for one hour. Return to the crock, and add the juice and "pulp" of the lemons and orange. Allow to stand till cool, then add wine yeast and the tannin, and yeast nutrient, since this is a liquor likely to be deficient in desirable elements. Let it remain closely covered for three days in a warm place, then strain into fermenting bottles and divide the raisins or concentrate equally amongst them. Fit trap. Leave until fermentation ceases and rack when wine clears. This wine, made in April or early May, is ready for drinking by Christmas, but improves vastly by being kept a further six months.

DANDELION WINE (2)

	British	Metric	U.S.A.
Dandelions	2 quarts	2 litres	2 quarts
Sugar	3 lb.	1½ kilos	2½ lb.
Oranges	4	4	4
Water	1 gallon	4½ litres	1 gallon
Yeast & nutrient			

This recipe makes a pleasant alternative to the foregoing one. It is important that the flowers should be picked in sunshine, or at midday, when they are fully opened, and the making of the wine should be done immediately.

Measure the yellow heads, discarding as much green as possible (without being too fussy about it), bringing the water to the boil meanwhile. Pour the boiling water over the flowers and leave them to steep for two days. Again, be careful not to exceed this time or a curious odour often invades and spoils what is a most pleasant table wine, properly made. Boil the mixture for 10 minutes with the orange peel (no white pith) and strain through muslin on the sugar, stirring to dissolve it. When cool add the yeast nutrient,

May

fruit juice and yeast. Put into fermentation jar and fit air-lock, and siphon off into clean bottles when the wine has cleared. It will be just right for drinking with your Christmas poultry!

FARMHOUSE TEA AND RAISIN WINE

	British	Metric	U.S.A.
Raisins (large)	2 lb.	1 kilo	1½ lb.
or Concentrate (white)	1 pint	560 mls.	1 pint
Wheat	1 lb.	½ kilo	¾ lb.
Tea	1 oz.	25 gms.	1 oz.
Sugar	2 lb.	1 kilo	1½ lb.
Lemons	4	4	4
Water	1 gallon	4½ litres	1 gallon
Yeast & nutrient			

Tie the tea loosely in a muslin bag. Pour the boiling water over it and let it mash, leaving it in the liquor until it is lukewarm. Remove the bag, and to the liquor add the chopped raisins or concentrate, wheat, sugar and sliced lemons. Add a Campden tablet. Dissolve 1 teaspoon of granulated yeast in the liquid and stir it in. Leave it to ferment in a closely-covered pan for 21 days, stirring often, then strain into fermenting bottle and fit air-lock. Siphon off into clean bottles when fermentation has ceased.

TEA WINE

	British	Metric	U.S.A.
Tea	4 tablesps.	4 tablesps.	6 tablesps.
Sugar	2½ lb.	1¼ kilos	2 lb.
Citric acid	2 teasps.	2 teasps.	3 teasps.
Water	1 gallon	4½ litres	1 gallon
Yeast & nutrient			

Some of the scented Indian and China teas make lovely wines. Pour the boiling water over the tea and sugar, stir well, and infuse until cool. Strain into fermenting jar, add acid, nutrient and yeast, and top up to bottom of neck with cold water. Fit an air-lock, ferment out, and rack and bottle as usual when stable. A clear, dry wine excellent for blending purposes.

May

RHUBARB WINE

If too much fruit is used rhubarb wine will contain an excess of oxalic acid, which is rather unpleasant, and it is best to keep the fruit content low and employ a "dry sugar" method of juice extraction invented by Mrs. Suzanne Tritton. The wine is best made in May; at other times of the year jellification sometimes seems to occur.

	British	Metric	U.S.A.
Rhubarb	3 lb.	1¼ kilos	2½ lb.
Sugar	3 lb.	1¼ kilos	2½ lb.
Water, to	1 gallon	4½ litres	1 gallon
Wine yeast & nutrient			

Do not peel the rhubarb but chop it, or slice it thinly· Cover the fruit with the dry sugar and leave it until most of the sugar has dissolved (at least 24 hours) then strain off. Stir the pulp in a little water and strain again, and with more water rinse out all remaining sugar into the liquor, and make up to 1 gallon with water. Add a good general-purpose wine yeast, and the usual nutrients. If you wish to preserve the rhubarb taste ferment on, but if you wish to make a wine tasting rather like hock add one crushed Campden tablet first.

This is an excellent wine for blending, since it will take up the flavour of any other and its own will be virtually lost.

MEAD

	British	Metric	U.S.A.
English honey	4 lb.	2 kilos	4 lb.
Orange	1	1	1
Lemon	1	1	1
Water	1 gallon	4½ litres	1 gallon
Yeast & nutrient; pectic enzyme			

Put the honey into the water and bring to the boil, then pour into a crock and allow to cool. Add the juice from the orange and lemon, and the yeast, preferably a Maury yeast, or all-purpose wine yeast, and nutrient.

N.B.—It is most important to add a good nutrient, since the honey is deficient in essential minerals. Pour into

May

fermentation vessel and fit air-lock. Allow to ferment to completion—this is liable to take much longer than with most country wines—and rack when no further bubbles are passing. Mead should preferably be matured for at least a year after this, but one needs to be very strong-willed to follow this advice!

HAWTHORN BLOSSOM WINE

	British	Metric	U.S.A.
Hawthorn blossom	2 quarts	2¼ litres	4 pints
Sugar	3½ lb.	1½ kilos	2¾ lb.
Lemons	2	2	2
Grape tannin	1 teasp.	1 teasp.	1 teasp.
Water	1 gallon	4½ litres	1 gallon
Yeast & nutrient			

Grate the rind from the lemons, being careful to include no white pith, and boil with the sugar and the juice of one lemon in the water for half an hour. Pour into a bowl and when it has cooled to 70°F. (21°C.) add the yeast (and, preferably, as with all flower wines, a good yeast nutrient). Leave for 24 hours, then tip in the flowers. Let the mixture stand for another eight days, stirring well each day. Then strain through two thicknesses of butter muslin into fermenting vessel, and fit air-lock. Rack for the first time when it clears and after a second racking about three months later (about six months in all) bottle in the usual way. This is a light and delicious wine.

LEMON THYME WINE

(By Mr. L. Foest, Penygraig House, Ammanford, Carns.)

	British	Metric	U.S.A.
Lemon thyme leaves	1 pint	½ litre	1 pint
Raisins	1 lb.	½ kilo	¾ lb.
or Concentrate (white)	½ pint	280 mls.	½ pint
Sugar	3 lb.	1½ kilos	2¼ lb.
Rhubarb	3 lb.	1½ kilos	2¼ lb.
Water	1 gallon	4½ litres	1 gallon
Yeast & nutrient			

May

Cut up the rhubarb into ½ in. lengths, and chop the lemon thyme (to approximately the size of mint when making mint sauce). Pour boiling water over them, and then add the raisins or concentrate. Stir every day for two weeks. Strain on to the sugar, stir thoroughly and add yeast, wine yeast, or a level teaspoonful of granulated yeast. Leave to ferment, closely covered and in a warm place, for another two weeks. Strain into fermenting vessel and fit air-lock, and leave until it has fermented right out. Ladies may prefer to add ½ lb.–1 lb. more sugar to obtain a much sweeter wine, but this is best done finally, to taste, and not at the outset.

NETTLE WINE

	British	Metric	U.S.A.
Young nettle tops	2 quarts	2 litres	4 pints
Sugar	4 lb.	1¾ kilos	3 lb.
Lemons	2	2	2
Root ginger	½ oz.	10 gms.	½ oz.
Water	1 gallon	4½ litres	1 gallon

Pick only the tops of the nettles, rinse them in water, and drain. Simmer them in some of the water with the bruised ginger and lemon peel (being careful to exclude any white pith) for 45 minutes. Strain, and make the liquor up to a gallon by adding more water. Pour this hot liquor over the sugar, add the juice of the lemons and the yeast nutrient, and stir until the sugar dissolves, and when the liquor has cooled to 70°F. (21°C.) add the yeast, preferably a general-purpose wine yeast. Keep the crock closely covered in a warm place, and after four days stir thoroughly and transfer the liquor to fermentation vessel and fit air-lock. When the wine begins to clear, rack off into fresh bottles, and leave for another three months before the final bottling.

May

SACK

Many, out of curiosity, want to try making sack, once a favourite English drink, mentioned by Shakespeare and earlier writers. It can be made as follows:

	British	Metric	U.S.A.
Fennel roots	3 or 4	3 or 4	3 or 4
Sprays of rue	3 or 4	3 or 4	3 or 4
Honey	4 lb.	1¾ kilos	3 lb.
Citric acid	1 dessertsp.	2 teasps.	1 tablesp.
Water	2 gallons	9 litres	2 gallons
Yeast & nutrient			

Wash the roots and leaves and boil them in the water for 45 minutes. Do not be tempted to add more fennel or you will get an unpleasantly strong flavour. Then pour the liquor through a nylon sieve and add the honey. Boil the whole for nearly two hours, skimming off any froth or scum which arises. Allow the liquor to cool to 70°F. (21°C.), then add your chosen yeast and yeast nutrient, and put into cask or fermenting jar and fit air-lock. Sack, like most meads, may be a little slow to ferment and mature, and it is important not to omit the yeast nutrient, or this will be aggravated. Rack after four months if the sack has cleared, if not, delay racking until it has. It is fit for drinking after a year.

VANILLA WINE

	British	Metric	U.S.A.
Rhubarb	6 lb.	2¾ kilos	5 lb.
Sugar	4 lb.	1¾ kilos	3 lb.
Lemons	2	2	2
Hawthorn Blossom	1 gallon	4½ litres	1 gallon
Water	1 gallon	4½ litres	1 gallon
Yeast & nutrient			

When boiling water is used in the making of rhubarb wine jellification is often caused later, during fermentation. It is safer, therefore, to employ a cold water method.

If cold water is used, of course, the natural yeasts present

May

in quantity (the bloom on the rhubarb) may complicate your ferment if you are using a wine yeast and it is therefore best to add a little sulphite (one Campden tablet per gallon) at the outset. Alternatively you may care in this case to ferment with the natural yeast (in this case, since there is so much of it present, the method usually works quite well). If you do, omit the Campden tablet, and add no yeast.

Cut the rhubarb into small pieces, cover with cold water, and add hawthorn flowers and the juice and rind of the two lemons, excluding any white pith. Add also one crushed Campden tablet. Keep the pan closely covered (**not** in a warm place) and stir daily for 10 days. Strain on to 2 lb. sugar, stir thoroughly until all sugar is dissolved, and add yeast. Keep in a warm place, closely covered. After four to five days add the remainder of the sugar, stirring thoroughly then transfer the liquor to fermenting jar and fit air-lock. Siphon off the lees after three months, and again three months later, when the wine may be bottled. At the second racking it will be vastly improved by the addition of up to ¼ pint of glycerine, to counter any over-acidity.

BALM WINE

	British	Metric	U.S.A.
Balm leaves (or small packet of dried balm)	2 quarts	2½ litres	4 pints
Raisins	1 lb.	½ kilo	¾ lb.
or Concentrate (white)	½ pint	280 mls.	½ pint
Sugar	3 lb.	1½ kilos	2½ lb.
Lemon	1	1	1
Orange	1	1	1
Grape tannin	1 teasp.	1 teasp.	1 teasp.
Water	1 gallon	4½ litres	1 gallon
Yeast & nutrient			

Add boiling water to the bruised leaves, raisins or concentrate, sugar and the juice and rinds of the lemon and oranges. When cool add yeast. Allow to work for seven days, then siphon into fermenting vessel with air-lock until fermentation is finished. The tender shoots should be used if aroma is considered of most importance.

103

May

ELDERFLOWER WINE

	British	Metric	U.S.A.
Elderflowers (not pressed down)	¾ pint	½ litre	¾ pint
or ½ oz. dried flowers			
Sugar	3½ lb.	1½ kilos	2¾ lb.
Raisins	½ lb.	¼ kilo	½ lb.
or Concentrate (white)	¼ pint	140 mls.	¼ pint
Lemons	3	3	3
Grape tannin	1 teasp.	1 teasp.	1 teasp.
Water	1 gallon	4½ litres	1 gallon

Gather the flowers on a sunny day when they are fully opened, and trim them from the stems with a pair of scissors, until you have ¾ pint (pressed down lightly) of petals. Bring the water to the boil and pour over the flowers, then add the sugar, chopped raisins or concentrate and lemon juice. When cool (70°F., 21°C.) add the yeast (a prepared wine yeast is best but granulated yeast can be used), your grape tannin, and nutrient. The nutrient is **most** important in this case. Cover well and leave to ferment in a warm place for four or five days. Strain into another jar, fit air-lock, and leave to ferment. When it clears, siphon it off the deposit for the first time; two months later rack it again, and bottle it.

SPARKLING ELDERFLOWER

The previous wine will be nearly dry but when it has started to clear, and while there is still some sugar present, it may prove suitable to convert into a sparkling wine. A bottle containing some of the wine is stood in a warm place and lightly plugged with cotton-wool. If after a week a slight yeast deposit has formed it is quite safe to transfer all the wine to champagne bottles which are either closed with corks well wired down or by screw caps similar to cider flagons. The bottles are stored on their sides in a cool place, and after six months or so should be sparkling and ready to drink. If, on the other hand, when trying the wine out for its suitability for bottle fermentation, a heavy yeast deposit is noted then fermentation must be continued for a few more days, or even weeks, till there is less sugar in the wine. A further test then

June

should show a smaller yeast deposit, in which case the wine can be bottled and complete its fermentation in the bottle. Bottling a wine which shows a heavy deposit will inevitably lead to burst bottles.

GREEN GOOSEBERRY WINE

	British	Metric	U.S.A.
Ripe green gooseberries	6 lb.	2½ kilos	5 lb.
Sugar	2½ lb.	1¼ kilos	2 lb.
Water	6–7 pints	3–4 litres	6–7 pints
Yeast & nutrient; pectic enzyme			

Top, tail and wash the gooseberries, put into large crock and squeeze by hand until they are pulpy. Add the enzyme and water and allow to stand for three days, well covered, stirring occasionally. Strain through two thicknesses of muslin, and add the sugar, stirring until it is all dissolved, then add yeast and yeast nutrient. Put into fermenting bottle and fit air-lock, leaving until bubbles cease to pass; then rack off and leave to mature, siphoning off the lees again after another six months. Leave for a year before drinking. Indistinguishable from a good hock.

WALLFLOWER WINE

	British	Metric	U.S.A.
Wallflower blossoms	1 pint	½ litre	1 pint
Large raisins or sultanas	½ lb.	¼ kilo	½ lb.
or Concentrate (white)	¼ pint	140 mls.	¼ pint
Sugar	2½ lb.	1¼ kilos	2 lb.
Lemons, juice	2	2	2
Grape tannin	1 teasp.	1 teasp.	1 teasp.
Water	1 gallon	4½ litres	1 gallon
Yeast & nutrient			

Put the sugar, minced sultanas, and flowerlets into a polythene bucket and pour over them 3 quarts hot (not boiling) water. Stir vigorously, when cool add the lemon juice tannin, and a general-purpose wine yeast, and ferment, well covered, for not more than three days. Strain into fermentation jar, top up with cold boiled water to bottom of neck, fit air-lock, and continue as usual. If desired grape concentrate can be substituted for the raisins or sultanas.

PANSY WINE

Using 3 pints of flowers, this can be made in the same way as wallflower wine.

PARSLEY WINE

	British	Metric	U.S.A.
Parsley, fresh	1 lb.	½ kilo	1 lb.
(or 1 small packet dried parsley)			
Sugar	4 lb.	1¾ kilos	3 lb.
Oranges	2	2	2
Lemons	2	2	2
Grape tannin	1 teasp.	1 teasp.	1 teasp.
Water	1 gallon	4½ litres	1 gallon
Yeast & nutrient; ½ oz. bruised ginger if desired			

Boil the parsley (the dried variety should firstly be infused for 24 hours), bruised ginger and thinly peeled rinds of the lemons and oranges for 20 minutes in the gallon of water. Strain on to the sugar and stir well. When lukewarm add the yeast and the fruit juice. Stir and cover, leave for 24 hours. Pour into a fermenting jar and insert an air-lock. Leave in a warm place to ferment to a finish. Siphon off into a storage jar.

SAGE WINE

	British	Metric	U.S.A.
Sage leaves	4 lb.	1¾ kilos	3 lb.
Minced large			
raisins	8 lb.	3½ kilos	6 lb.
or Concentrate (white)	3 pints	1 litre	3 pints
Barley	1 lb.	½ kilo	¾ lb.
Lemons	2	2	2
Water	1 gallon	4½ litres	1 gallon
Yeast & nutrient			

Pour the boiling water onto the raisins (or concentrate) and barley and add the chopped leaves of the red sage. Allow to cool and then add the juice of the two lemons and the nutrient and prepared wine yeast or a level teaspoonful of dried yeast. Keep covered, in a warm place, for seven days, stirring daily, then place in a fermentation vessel with an air-lock and ferment in the usual way.

June

BRAMBLE TIP WINE

	British	Metric	U.S.A.
Bramble tip	1 gallon	4½ litres	1 gallon
Sugar	3 lb.	1½ kilos	2¼ lb.
Citric acid	1 teasp.	1 teasp.	1 teasp.
Grape tannin	1 teasp.	1 teasp.	1 teasp.
Water	1 gallon	4½ litres	1 gallon

Place the tips in a crock and cover them with boiling water. Leave this to stand overnight, then bring to the boil and simmer gently for a quarter of an hour. Strain through muslin on to the sugar, add the yeast when it has cooled, and keep closely covered in a warm place for 10 days. Then pour into fermenting jar and fit air-lock. Leave until wine clears, then siphon off and bottle.

OAKLEAF OR WALNUT WINE

	British	Metric	U.S.A.
Oak or walnut leaves	1 gallon	4½ litres	1 gallon
Sugar	3½ lb.	1½ kilos	2¼ lb.
Lemons, juice	2	2	2
Water	1 gallon	4½ litres	1 gallon
Yeast & nutrient			

Bring 4–6 pints of the water to the boil and dissolve the sugar on it; when it clears pour, boiling, over the leaves. Infuse overnight, and next day strain into fermenting jar. Add the lemon juice, nutrient and yeast and shake well. Top up to bottom of neck with cold water, and then ferment out in a warm place. Rack when it clears, and again two months later.

BLACKCURRANT, RED-CURRANT OR WHITE-CURRANT WINE

	British	Metric	U.S.A
Black-, red- or white-currants	3 lb.	1½ kilos	2¼ lb.
Sugar	3½ lb.	1¾ kilos	2½ lb.
Water	1 gallon	4½ litres	1 gallon
Yeast & nutrient; pectic enzyme			

107

July

Put the currants into a large earthenware jar and crush them. Boil up the sugar in the water and pour, still boiling, on to the currants. When it has cooled to about blood heat, add the pectic enzyme and a day later a wine yeast, and keep closely covered for five days in a warm place, giving it an occasional stir. Then strain into a fermenting jar, fit air-lock. Let it stand until fermentation ceases and the wine clears, usually in about three months, then siphon off into fresh, sterilised bottles.

BLACKCURRANT, RIBENA WINE

One 12-oz. bottle of Ribena Blackcurrant juice will in fact make one gallon of wine. Dissolve 3 lb. of sugar in some warm water, and add the blackcurrant juice. Bring to the boil and simmer for 10 minutes to drive off any preservative, cool, and pour into a gallon jar, filling it to the shoulder. Then add your chosen wine yeast, or a level teaspoon of Heath and Heather granulated yeast. The merest trace of acid (one-third of a teaspoon of citric acid) and a pinch of yeast nutrient should also be added. Insert the air-lock and stand the jar in a warm place for fermentation to get under way. When the first vigorous fermentation has died down after a fortnight or so, top up the jar with water to the bottom of the neck, and re-insert air-lock; then continue with the fermentation in the usual way.

BROAD BEAN WINE

. . . and you just **must** try this most unusual and astonishing wine for which the recipe comes from Mr. C. J. Padwick, of 16 Clarendon Avenue, Andover. This recipe produces a light dry wine of superb quality, hard as that may be to believe!

	British	Metric	U.S.A.
Broad beans (shelled)	4 lb.	2 kilos	3 lb.
Sugar	2¾ lb.	1½ kilos	2 lb.
Raisins	¼ lb.	100 gms.	¼ lb.
or Concentrate (white)	4 oz.	100 mls.	4 oz.
Lemon	1	1	1
Water	1 gallon	4½ litres	1 gallon
Yeast & nutrient			

July

Mr. Padwick writes: Use beans that are too old for normal culinary purposes. To 4 lb. of shelled beans add one gallon of water and boil slowly for one hour. It is essential that the skins do not break or you will have difficulty in clearing the wine. Strain off the liquor and make up to one gallon with boiled water. For a dry wine add 2¾ lb. of sugar, the juice of one lemon and ¼ lb. of raisins or concentrate. When sufficiently cooled add the yeast, and allow five days for the first fermentation. Remove the raisins after this period, fix the air-lock and from then on treat as any other wine. By careful use of the hydrometer more sugar can be added at stages, but I do not recommend this as a sweet wine.

CHERRY WINE

	British	Metric	U.S.A.
Black cherries	6 lb.	2¾ kilos	5 lb.
Sugar	4½ lb.	2 kilos	3 lb.
Citric acid	1 teasp.	1 teasp.	1 teasp.
Water	1 gallon	4½ litres	1 gallon
Yeast & nutrient			

Crush the cherries (without breaking the stones) and then pour the boiling water over them. Leave to soak for 48 hours. Strain through two thicknesses of muslin. Bring the juice just to boiling point and pour it over the sugar.

Stir until the sugar is dissolved. Allow to cool and then stir in the yeast nutrient. Cover closely and ferment in a warm place for 14 days, then put into fermenting bottle and fit air-lock. Siphon off when finished and clear into clean bottles.

HONEYSUCKLE WINE

	British	Metric	U.S.A.
Honeysuckle blossom (pressed down lightly)	2 pints	1 litre	2 pints
Sugar	3 lb.	1½ kilos	2¼ lb.
Raisins	¼ lb.	100 gms.	¼ lb.
or Concentrate (white)	4 ozs.	100 mls.	4 ozs.
Lemon	1	1	1
Orange	1	1	1
Campden tablet	1	1	1
Grape tannin	1 teasp.	1 teasp.	1 teasp.
Water	1 gallon	4½ litres	1 gallon
Yeast & nutrient			

109

July

The flowers must be fully open, and dry. Wash them in a colander, pour the water (cold) over them, and stir in 2 lb. of sugar, the minced raisins (or concentrate), and the citrus fruit juice. Add the crushed Campden tablet. Stir well, and next day add the yeast (a Sauternes is suitable), tannin and nutrients. Ferment for a week in a warm place, stirring daily, then add the remaining sugar and stir well. Strain into fermenting jar and ferment, rack and bottle as usual. Use ½ lb. sugar less for a really dry wine.

MARIGOLD WINE

	British	Metric	U.S.A.
Marigold flowers (no stalks)	3 quarts	3 litres	3 quarts
Sugar	3 lb.	1½ kilos	2¼ lb.
Lemons	2	2	2
Water	1 gallon	4½ litres	1 gallon

Bring the water to the boil, dissolve the sugar in it, and allow to cool. Add the crushed flowers, the juice and rind of the lemons (being careful to include no white pith), the yeast nutrient, and yeast (prepared wine yeast or a level teaspoonful of dried yeast). Leave in a warm place, closely covered, for a week, stirring twice daily, then strain into a fermenting jar, insert an air-lock, and leave in a fairly warm place to finish. When fermentation ceases and wine has cleared, siphon off into clean bottles and keep in a cool place for at least six months before drinking.

MARROW WINE

Although the recipe which advocates filling a marrow with brown sugar to make Marrow Rum is one which appeals by its novelty I have never yet tasted any made by this method which has been successful, unless the recipe has been considerably adjusted. Usually the result is far too sweet. You will find this recipe for Marrow Wine far more successful.

	British	Metric	U.S.A.
Ripe marrow flesh	5 lb.	2¼ kilos	4 lb.
White sugar	3 lb.	2 kilos	2¼ lb.
(or brown if you wish a rum colour)			
Lemons	2	2	2
Oranges	2	2	2
Root ginger	1 oz.	25 gms.	1 oz.
Water	1 gallon	4½ litres	1 gallon
Yeast & nutrient; pectic enzyme			

Grate the marrow and use the seeds, slice the oranges and lemons, bruise the ginger, and put all into a jug or crock. Pour over the boiling water and when cool add enzyme, yeast and nutrient. Leave five days, closely covered, stirring frequently, strain and dissolve the sugar in the liquid. Either put into a fermentation jar and fit air-lock, or keep it closely covered and then ferment in the usual way. When it clears siphon it off the yeast. It should be ready after about six months and can then be bottled.

MEADOWSWEET WINE

	British	Metric	U.S.A.
Meadowsweet flowers	1 gallon	4½ litres	1 gallon
(heads only or 1 small packet dried heads)			
Sugar	3 lb.	1½ kilos	2¼ lb.
Grape tannin	1 teasp.	1 teasp.	1 teasp.
Citric acid	1 dessertsp.	2 teasps.	1 tablesp.
Raisins	1 lb.	½ kilo	¾ lb.
or Concentrate	½ pint	280 mls.	½ pint
Water	1 gallon	4½ litres	1 gallon
Yeast & nutrient			

Place the flowers, chopped fruit and sugar in polythene vessel, pour in the concentrate and boiling water, and stir well. When cool add the citric acid, tannin and yeast nutrient. Introduce the wine yeast and ferment on the pulp for 10 days, stirring twice daily and keeping it closely covered. Then strain into fermentation vessel and ferment, rack, and bottle in due course.

July

MORELLO CHERRY WINE

	British	Metric	U.S.A.
Morello cherries (cracked or windfall)	8 lb.	4 kilos	6 lb.
Sugar	3½ lb.	1½ kilos	2½ lb.
Water	1 gallon	4½ litres	1 gallon
Yeast & nutrient; pectic enzyme			

Stalk and wash the fruit, place in a crock, and add one pint of cold water to each pound of fruit, and then one crushed Campden tablet and enzyme. Lastly, add a level teaspoonful of dried yeast. Leave for 10 days, keeping closely covered, but stir well each day and mash the fruit with the hands.

To strain it is a good plan to tie muslin over another pan, tying it on. Then by standing a colander on two laths over this, the bulk of the fruit is retained in the colander and the liquor enabled to strain through the muslin more easily. Do not squeeze or hurry the process.

Measure the liquid, and to each quart add 1 lb. sugar; stir well till dissolved. Leave for four days in a warm place, still covered, then put into fermenting bottle and fit air-lock. When fermentation has finished and wine has cleared, rack off into clean bottles and keep six months before using.

PLUM WINE

Most plums will make good wine, but generally speaking Victoria plums have been found to be the most satisfactory. Even they sometimes produce a wine which is somewhat lacking in body, and many winemakers, to counter this plum failing, are in the habit of adding a pound of grain (wheat or barley) to the recipe.

	British	Metric	U.S.A.
Plums	6 lb.	2¾ kilos	5 lb.
Sugar	3½ lb.	1½ kilos	2½ lb.
Water	1 gallon	4½ litres	1 gallon
Yeast & nutrient; pectic enzyme			

Cut the plums in half, and crush them in your hands. Take half of the water, bring it to the boil, and then pour it over the fruit "pulp". Leave it four or five hours, then add the other half of the water (cold) and the pectic enzyme. Leave for 48 hours, then strain, and you should have about a gallon of really clear juice. Bring this to the boil, and then pour it over the sugar, stirring to dissolve. Allow the liquor to cool to 70°F. (21°C.) then add the yeast (preferably a Bordeaux, Tokay or Sauternes yeast or a level teaspoon of granulated yeast), pour the whole into your fermenting vessel, and fit an air-lock. When the wine begins to clear, siphon it off for the first time, and when *all* fermentation has finished, rack it again into clean bottles and cork.

RASPBERRY WINE

If ever you can persuade yourself *not* to eat raspberries, but to make wine with them instead, here is an excellent recipe:

	British	Metric	U.S.A.
Raspberries	4 lb.	1¾ kilos	2½ lb.
Sugar	3½ lb.	1½ kilos	2½ lb.
Water	1 gallon	4½ litres	1 gallon
Yeast & nutrient			

Bring the water to the boil and pour it over the fruit; then leave it to cool. Mash the fruit well with the hands, and add pectic enzme, then cover it closely and leave for four days, stirring daily. Strain through at least two thicknesses of butter muslin on to the sugar, and stir thoroughly to dissolve. Add a good wine yeast (Burgundy, Port or Sauternes is best), or a level teaspoon of granulated yeast, and stir well in. Leave for 24 hours, closely covered, in a warm place, then put the liquor into your fermentation vessel, and fit air-lock. Ferment it right out, and when it clears, siphon the wine off the lees into clean bottles.

RASPBERRY AND RED-CURRANT WINE

	British	Metric	U.S.A.
Raspberries	4 lb.	1¾ kilos	3 lb.
Red-currants	4 lb.	1¾ kilos	3 lb.
Sugar	4 lb.	1¾ kilos	3 lb.
Water	about 6 pints	3½ litres	about 6 pints
Yeast & nutrient			

August

Wash the fruit, rejecting any which are damaged, and press out all the juice. (If a press is not available use a plate and colander stood on laths over a crock.) Boil the squeezed "pulp" in three times its own volume of water for two hours, and then strain on to the original juice. The "pulp" should be squeezed dry and this liquid also added. Measure the total liquid thus obtained and to each gallon add 4 lb. sugar, and then put the yeast (when the liquor has cooled to blood heat). Put into fermenting bottle, filling to shoulder to allow space for the vigour of the primary fermentation, but keep a little liquor aside in a covered jug with which to "top up" once the initial ferment is over. Fit air-lock and leave until fermentation is finished. Then siphon off and keep for six months before the final bottling.

ROSE PETAL WINE

Many gardens have masses of rose petals which, in the normal course of events, would finish up on the compost heap. But why not take advantage of their glorious scent and make this most unusual wine? All you need is:

	British	Metric	U.S.A.
Rose petals	2 quarts	2 litres	2 quarts
(the stronger scented the better)			
Sugar	2½ lb.	1¼ kilos	2 lb.
Lemons	2	2	2
Water	1 gallon	4½ litres	1 gallon
Grape concentrate	½ pint	280 mls.	½ pint
Yeast & nutrient			

Bring the water to the boil, and add the sugar, rose petals, the small quantity of grape juice concentrate and juice of the lemon. Stir well, and when it has cooled to 70°F. (21°C.) add the yeast (a G.P. wine yeast or a level teaspoon of granulated yeast and a yeast nutrient). Leave to ferment for a week, stirring daily, and keeping closely covered. Then strain into a fermentation jar and ferment until finished. A wine made in this way will normally have a good colour, if coloured roses are used; if less colour is required the petals should be strained from the liquor three days earlier.

August

STRAWBERRY WINE

	British	Metric	U.S.A.
Strawberries	4 lb.	2 kilos	3 lb.
Sugar	3 lb.	1½ kilos	2¼ lb.
Citric acid	1 teasp.	5 gms.	1 teasp.
Grape tannin	½ teasp.	½ teasp.	½ teasp.
Water	1 gallon	4½ litres	1 gallon
Yeast & nutrient			

Take the stems from the strawberries, and wash the fruit. Mash the berries well, and mix with the sugar and 2 quarts water. Leave for 24–36 hours, then strain liquor into fermenting jar; add a further quart of water to the pulp, mix well, and immediately strain again, then add the acid, tannin, yeast nutrient and yeast, and make up to 1 gallon with cold water. Stir thoroughly, fit air-lock, and continue as usual.

BURNET WINE

	British	Metric	U.S.A.
Burnet flowers	2 quarts	2 litres	2 quarts
Sugar	1 lb.	½ kilo	¾ lb.
Honey	1 lb.	½ kilo	¾ lb.
Raisins	1 lb.	½ kilo	¾ lb.
or Concentrate (red)	½ pint	280 mls.	½ pint
Lemon	1	1	1
Orange	1	1	1
Water	1 gallon	4½ litres	1 gallon
Yeast & nutrient			

The Greater Salad Burnet, *Sanguisorba Officinalis*, is not found much in the south, but is fairly plentiful in the damp meadows of the northern counties, and makes a pleasant, light, rosé wine. The plant, however, is rather uncooperative, since it opens its blooms in succession up the stem, so that only one zone of flowers is open at the same time. To outwit the plant, pick as many as possible of the flowers as they open, placing them in a bowl of water to infuse. As the other blooms open, they can be added to the first, until half a gallon of blossoms has been picked.

Let these stand for seven days after the last flower has been added, then strain the water on to the sugar, clear honey,

115

August

and well chopped raisins or concentrate. Add the juice and a little of the rinds of a lemon and an orange, and simmer for 20 minutes. Strain into a gallon jar, leaving a little of the liquor for the preparation of a starter. When this is working well, and the liquor in the jar is lukewarm, stir in the starter, top up the jar with cold water, if necessary, and leave to ferment, closely covered.

GOLDEN ROD WINE

Method as for Gorse Wine (see April, page 95).

CARROT WINE

. . . a readily available and very popular drink, with both "kick" and flavour . . .

	British	Metric	U.S.A.
Carrots	6 lb.	2¾ kilos	5 lb.
Wheat	1 lb.	½ kilo	¾ lb.
Sugar	4 lb.	1¾ kilos	3 lb.
Lemons	2	2	2
Oranges	2	2	2
Raisins	1 tablesp.	1 tablesp.	2 tablesp.
or Concentrate	4 ozs.	100 mls.	4 ozs.
Water	1 gallon	4½ litres	1 gallon
Yeast & nutrient			

Wash the carrots well but do not peel. Put into the water and bring to the boil; then simmer gently until the carrots are very tender. Use the carrots for food, and strain the water. Make up to one gallon. In a bowl put the sugar, sliced oranges and lemons and pour over the hot liquid. Stir until the sugar is dissolved, and then stand until luke-warm. Then add the chopped raisins (or concentrate) and wheat and sprinkle the level teaspoonful of granulated yeast on top. Leave to ferment, closely covered, for 15 days, stirring daily. Then skim, strain and put into fermenting jar. Fit air-lock and leave until it is clear and stable. Then bottle. Keep almost a year (from the start of the fermentation) before drinking.

August

"FOLLY" OR VINE PRUNINGS WINE

Those of you who are growing vines—and all amateur winemakers should, or they miss a great deal of fun and enjoyment—will have not only grapes (in September) but, throughout the summer, a plentiful supply of vine prunings and leaves as the growing vines are cut back to ensure that the maximum nutrition goes into the bunches of grapes. Do not waste these prunings and leaves; they will make excellent wine! Cut only the green shoots and not ripe wood or the vine will "bleed".

	British	Metric	U.S.A.
Leaves and tendrils	5 lb.	2¼ kilos	4 lb.
Sugar	3 lb.	1½ kilos	2¼ lb.
Citric acid	1 teasp.	1 teasp.	1 teasp.
Water	1 gallon	4½ litres	1 gallon
Yeast & nutrient			

Put the cuttings and leaves into a bowl and pour on to them the boiling water. Let this stand for 48 hours, but turn occasionally to submerge top leaves and keep prunings well under water. Keep crock closely covered. Pour off liquid and press out remaining leaves and tendrils. "Wash" the leaves with a pint of water and press again. Dissolve the sugar in the liquid, add the yeast and yeast nutrient, and pour into fermenting vessel and fit air-lock. Ferment right out in the usual way and siphon off when clear.

POMEGRANATE WINE

	British	Metric	U.S.A.
Pomegranates	10	10	10
Barley	¼ lb.	¼ kilo	¼ lb.
Sugar	3 lb.	1½ kilos	2¼ lb.
Lemon	1	1	1
Water	1 gallon	4½ litres	1 gallon
Yeast & nutrient			

Clean the outer skins of the pomegranates and meanwhile bring the water to the boil, with the barley in it. Simmer for about five minutes; then strain on to the chopped

August

pomegranates, the sugar, and the juice of the lemon. Stir well. When cool add the nutrient and yeast. Ferment, closely covered, on the pulp for five days, then strain into fermenting jar. Bottle the wine when it clears. An excellent medium table wine.

GINGER BEER

If you wish to be popular with the kiddies during the holidays, try making them some ginger beer . . .

	British	Metric	U.S.A.
Well-bruised root ginger	1¼ ozs.	25 gms.	1 oz.
Sugar	1 lb.	½ kilo	¾ lb.
Lemons	2	2	2
Cream of tartar	¼ teasp.	¼ teasp.	¼ teasp.
Water	1 gallon	4½ litres	1 gallon
Yeast & nutrient			

Put into a large bowl or jar the sugar, the rinds (thinly peeled), add the juice of the two lemons, and the well-bruised ginger. Add the squeezed halves of the lemons to the water as it comes to the boil. When it reaches boiling point, pour it over the ingredients in the bowl. Remove lemon halves, stir well and cover. When tepid add the yeast, previously dissolved in a small amount of the warm liquid. Use a small bottle for this, dropping crumbled yeast in and shaking it to dissolve; leave it half-an-hour or more before adding it to the liquor. Lastly, stir in the cream of tartar. Cover and leave for 24 hours. Strain and bottle, and tie down the corks. NEVER use screwstoppers or the bottles may burst. Store in a cool place and drink fairly soon. Take care when opening the bottles, or they are apt to froth over.

PEACH PERFECTION

This is a recipe by the late Mrs. Cherry Leeds, of Twickenham, for a peach wine which is so superb—and *cheap* —that we give the fullest possible instructions . . .

It sounds extravagant, but it is not. Keep an eye on the greengrocers and you'll see that in August (usually about the first fortnight) peaches come right down in price, to only a few pence each. The wine works out at about 7½p a bottle. Mrs. Leeds used a Kitzinger sherry or Tokay yeast.

TO MAKE 10 GALLONS

	British	Metric	U.S.A.
Peaches	30 lb.	13½ kilos	25 lb.
Sugar, white	22 lb.	10 kilos	18 lb.
Sugar, brown	10 lb.	4½ kilos	8 lb.
Citric acid	3 ozs.	75 gms.	3 ozs.
Grape tannin	1½ teasp.	1½ teasp.	1½ teasp.
Water	10 gallons	45 litres	10 gallons

Yeast & nutrient; pectic enzyme

Wipe peaches and remove the stones; drop into large container such as a polythene bin. Scrub hands well and squeeze the peaches until well washed. Well cover with boiling water and leave covered overnight.

The next day stir in the Pectic enzyme and cover well. On the third day strain through muslin, twice if possible to reduce sludge, and put into the 10-gallon jar; add citric acid, tannin and nutrient.

At this point it is a simple matter to place the jar or carboy into the position it will occupy during fermentation. Put 20 lb. of sugar into the large container and add sufficient boiling water to dissolve, and when cool add to the jar. Then the level of the liquid is brought up to the turn of the shoulder of the jar with boiled water. Open the yeast bottle, pour in, and re-fit air-lock. The gravity at this stage will be about 100; the original gravity is almost invariably 25–30. Fermentation will start on the third day if the temperature is sufficient (70–75°F., 21–24°C.).

The rest of the sugar is added in stages from now on, the first addition of four pints of syrup when the gravity is 30, that is, roughly, after two weeks. The sugar is then added in two-pint lots when the gravity is between 10 and 15 each time. The syrup used is 2 lb. sugar to one pint boiling water and cooled, thus making two pints syrup.

The fermenting period lasts for about seven or eight months, though one can keep it going for a year with small additions of syrup.

August

The first racking takes place when all the sugar is in and the reading is 10. Some of the wine will have to be removed to accommodate the last two pints of syrup. Stir up the jar and remove half a gallon. Put it by, under an air-lock, and this can be used to top up the jar after the first racking. Stir the liquid vigorously with an oak rod once a day for the first few weeks.

Because of the Pectinol used the wine will clear perfectly and after the first racking will become crystal clear, but don't be tempted to rack again until fermentation has ceased finally. This usually happens when the gravity is about five.

TO MAKE 5 GALLONS

For the 5-gallon jars use half quantities except the Pectic enzyme—this is 2 ozs.—otherwise the procedure is the same.

TO MAKE 1 GALLON

	British	Metric	U.S.A.
Peaches	3 lb.	1½ kilos	2¼ lb.
Sugar	3 lb.	1½ kilos	2¼ lb.
Citric acid	1 teasp.	1 teasp.	1 teasp.
Grape tannin	½ teasp.	½ teasp.	½ teasp.
Boiling water	1 gallon	4½ litres	1 gallon
Yeast & nutrient; pectic enzyme			

The method is the same but the yeast starter bottle is prepared on the same day as mashing, and the sugar is put in all together, just before the yeast starter.

APRICOT WINE: As Peach

PEA POD WINE

Despite its somewhat unattractive and prosaic name (a chance here for someone to invent a better one!), this is a light attractive wine which is a great favourite with many winemakers. Certainly no one can complain that the ingredients are expensive!

	British	Metric	U.S.A.
Pea pods	5 lb.	2¼ kilos	4 lb.
Sugar	3 lb.	1½ kilos	2¼ lb.
Citric acid	1 tablesp.	1 tablesp.	2 tablesp.
Grape tannin	½ teasp.	½ teasp.	½ teasp.
Water	1 gallon	4½ litres	1 gallon
Yeast & nutrient			

120

August

Wash the pods carefully, and then boil them in the water until they are tender, then strain and dissolve the sugar in the warm liquid. Add the yeast, and other ingredients, pour into jar, and fit air-lock. Siphon off when wine begins to clear and bottle when fermentation has ceased.

GREENGAGE WINE

	British	Metric	U.S.A.
Plums or greengages	4 lb.	1¾ kilos	3 lb.
Barley	¼ lb.	¼ kilo	¼ lb.
Sugar	4 lb.	1¾ kilos	3 lb.
Water	1 gallon	4½ litres	1 gallon
Yeast & nutrient; pectic enzyme			

Grind the barley in a mincer and cut up the fruit, putting both into a crock. Pour over them the boiling water, cover closely and leave for four days, adding the pectic enzyme when cool. Stir daily. Then strain through muslin on to the sugar, add the yeast nutrient and stir till all is dissolved. Then add the yeast (preferably a Burgundy wine yeast, but failing that a general-purpose wine yeast or a level teaspoonful of granulated yeast). Keep closely covered in a warm place for a week, then pour into fermenting bottle, filling to bottom of neck and fit air-lock. Siphon off for the ffrst time when it clears but do not bottle until assured that fermentation has completely finished.

BULLACE, DAMSON AND PLUM WINES
Method and quantities as for Greengage

RED GOOSEBERRY

	British	Metric	U.S.A.
Red gooseberries	4 lb.	1¾ kilos	3 lb.
Sugar	3 lb.	1½ kilos	2¼ lb.
Water	1 gallon	4½ litres	1 gallon
Yeast & nutrient; pectic enzyme			

Pick the ripe gooseberries on a dry day, choosing large and juicy fruits. Top and tail and mash well in a bowl before adding the enzyme and yeast. Pour on the cold water and

September

allow to stand three days, stirring twice a day. Strain well through nylon net and dissolve the sugar in the juice. Then put into fermenting jar and fit trap and leave until wine has cleared and fermented out. Then siphon off into clean bottles and cork.

PASSION FRUIT WINE

And this doesn't mean what you're thinking! The Passion Fruit, or Purple Granadilla, is of the *Passifloraceae*. The *Passiflora*, or Passion Flower, is so called because its several parts symbolise the story of the Passion of Our Lord. Two types produce edible fruit—*P. edulis* and *P. quadrangularis*, rather like plums.

	British	Metric	U.S.A.
Passion fruit	4 lb.	2 kilos	3 lb.
Barley	½ lb.	¼ kilo	½ lb.
Sugar	3½ lb.	1½ kilos	2½ lb.
Water	1 gallon	4½ litres	1 gallon
Yeast & nutrient; pectic enzyme			

As for Plum Wine.

APPLE WINE (1)

This is a truly delicious wine, and although apparently heavy on fruit is well worth making. It is strong, yet delicately flavoured, with an attractive, faintly "cidery" bouquet.

	British	Metric	U.S.A.
Apples (mixed windfalls)	24 lb.	10 kilos	18 lb.
Sugar (to the gallon of liquor)	3 lb.	1½ kilos	2¼ lb.
Water	1 gallon	4½ litres	1 gallon

Chop the apples into small pieces, put into a bowl, add the yeast and water (the water will not cover the apples). Leave for about a week, stirring vigorously several times a day to bring the apples at the bottom to the top. Keep the pan closely covered and in a fairly warm place. Then strain the juice from the apple "pulp". Press the juice from the apples and add to the rest of the liquor. To every gallon add

3 lb. of sugar. Put into cask or glass fermenting vessel and fit air-lock, racking when it has cleared. The wine will be ready for drinking within six months, but improves for being kept a year.

If eating apples are used it is a good idea to make every 10th pound one of crab apples, and another improvement is to employ a Sauternes wine yeast.

APPLE WINE (2)

	British	Metric	U.S.A.
Apples	6 lb.	2¾ kilos	5 lb.
Sugar	3 lb.	1½ kilos	2¼ lb.
Chopped raisins	½ lb.	¼ kilo	½ lb.
or Concentrate (white)	¼ pint	140 mls.	¼ pint
Lemon	1	1	1
Water	1 gallon	4½ litres	1 gallon
Yeast & nutrient			

Wash and cut up the apples, skins, brown patches and all. Windfalls will do. Simmer 10–15 minutes in one gallon of water. Strain liquid on to the sugar, and the thinly peeled rind of the lemon. Stir well. When lukewarm add the juice of the lemon, the yeast and the yeast nutrient to the liquid, and the concentrate if used in place of the raisins, cover and leave for 24 hours in a warm place, then pour into a fermenting jar, cover with three layers of clean nylon material, or insert air-lock. Leave in a warm place to ferment for four weeks. Siphon off into clean dry storage jar, and add the chopped raisins. Leave six months to mature under air-lock. Then siphon off into clean bottles, and cork.

ELDERBERRY WINE

	British	Metric	U.S.A.
Elderberries	3 lb.	1½ kilos	2¼ lb.
Sugar	3½ lb.	1½ kilos	2½ lb.
Water	1 gallon	4½ litres	1 gallon
Yeast & nutrient			

Strip the berries from the stalks by using the prongs of an ordinary table fork (otherwise it is a messy and tedious business), then weigh them and crush them in a bowl. Pour on the boiling water, and then let it cool to about 70°F.

September

(21°C.) before adding the yeast. Leave three days, stirring daily, then strain through muslin on to the sugar. Pour the liquid into a stone jar or dark glass bottle (in clear bottles the wine will lose its colour), but do not fill completely until first vigorous ferment has subsided, plugging the neck with cotton-wool. When the ferment is quieter fill to bottom of neck, and fit air-lock. Leave until fermentation is complete— it may be longer than most—then siphon off into clean, dark bottles and keep for six months at least.

GRAPE WINE

More and more people are now growing their own outdoor wine grapes, particularly in the South of England, and *The Amateur Winemaker* has received many requests for "grape wine recipes". The word grape here is really superfluous, since true wine can only be the product of the grape, as the etymology of the word shows (Greek *oine*-vine, *oinos*-wine) and it is fitting that in any book on wine the grape should have pride of place. Many are puzzled as to how to convert their grapes into wine, but in essentials nothing could be simpler.

Firstly, make sure that your grapes are as ripe as possible (the birds will tell you when they are nearly ready, if the vine is unprotected!), gather them, and set to work quickly. All one has to do is to ferment the grape juice, but it is as well to note that, if making small quantities, with a consequent high degree of wastage, as much as between 12 and 15 lb. of grapes will be required to produce one gallon of wine. About 4 lb. will make one bottle. And, even in one of our sunniest summers, when the sugar content of our grapes will perhaps be higher than usual, it is likely that one must expect to have to add some sugar, if a reasonably strong wine is required. If you use a hydrometer, it is simple to ascertain how much, but if you do not, no matter; the solution then is to aim at a strong wine, say 12-14% of alcohol by volume, and to continue adding the sugar in small quantities of, say 4 oz. to the gallon at a time, until the ferment is carried as far as it will go, and the sweetness of the wine is to your taste.

September

Many beginners seem to be puzzled by the difference between white wine and red, and ask whether black grapes can be employed to produce the former. The answer is: Yes. White wine can be made from grapes of either colour, the method being to express the juice and ferment it alone. Red wine, on the other hand, is produced by leaving the skins of the crushed black grapes in the "must", so that the colour from them is extracted.

If the skins are left in only one or two days a vine rosé will be produced, if longer a wine of much deeper colour. This process can usually be continued for about 10 days, but it is unwise to leave it much longer, and the liquid should then be drawn off.

A press, of course, is invaluable, and essential if making large quantities of white wine, but most winemakers will be able to contrive to press enough grapes for one or two gallons without one, by crushing with the hands or a piece of hard wood, or by using boards and weights, or some similar device. For white wine, of ocurse, the grapes must be contained in stout calico or some such material to keep the skins separate.

Aim at a strength of 12-14% alcohol by volume. If using a hydrometer, express the juice from a few of the grapes and measure the S.G. With English grapes it is likely to be fairly low, about 50 or 60, and to obtain the desired strength you will need to add 15-20 oz. of sugar. It may be higher, if so, consult the table overleaf, given by E. Chancrin in *Le Vin*.

(If you have no hydrometer, make a mental note of the fact that you are likely to have to add *up to* 2 lb. of sugar to each gallon, but do it by stages, adding 8 ozs. initially and thereafter 4 oz. at a time.)

If you are making wine from grapes for the first time it is unlikely that you will want to bother your head unduly about acidity, for **if the grapes are really ripe** any slight over-acidity can be masked by a little extra sugar once the wine is made. But for the perfectionist it is as well to note

125

September

that grapes—and certainly English grapes—are likely to be slightly too acid, and probably contain about 1.30% acid, whereas the desirable acidity is about 0.75%. The experienced winemaker will go to the trouble of correcting this by diluting with syrup, but for our present purpose this is an unnecessary complication.

S.G. of grape juice	Approx. number of ounces of sugar to be added to one gallon to increase alcohol (by volume) to:		
	10%	14%	18%
1050	11	20	32
1055	9	17	29
1060	7	15	27
1065	5	13	25
1070	3	11	23
1075	..	10	21
1080	..	8	20
1085	..	6	18
1090	..	4	16
1095	..	2	14
1100	..	..	12
1105	..	..	10
1110	..	..	8
1115	..	..	6
1120	..	..	4
1125	..	..	2
1130	..	..	..

WHITE WINE

Discard any mouldy or unsound grapes, remove the stems, and express the juice by means of a press or by crushing with the hands, the fruit being in a calico or sacking bag. If using a press, apply pressure gradually; it is better to repeat the pressing once or twice slowly, than to try to force it through, for you may only burst the bag and be in trouble.

ABOVE: Pleasant job this! . . . . . taking samples in the winery, using a "wine thief".

BELOW: Casks need to be checked rather more often.

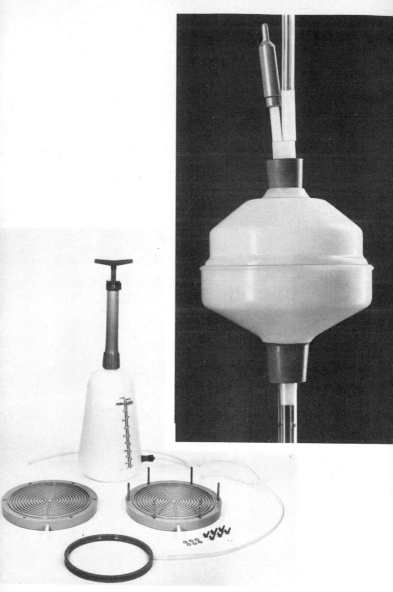

Two extremely efficient filters, the Vinamat (left) and the Harris.

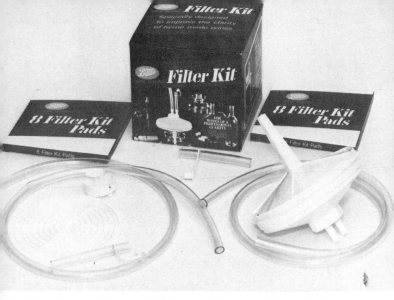

Two other excellent and very reasonably priced filters, that sold by Boots (above) and the Vinbrite, sold by Southern Vinyards below.

Cleanliness is all-important. A good cleansing-sterilising agent, a bottle brush and a draining rack make bottle-washing easier.

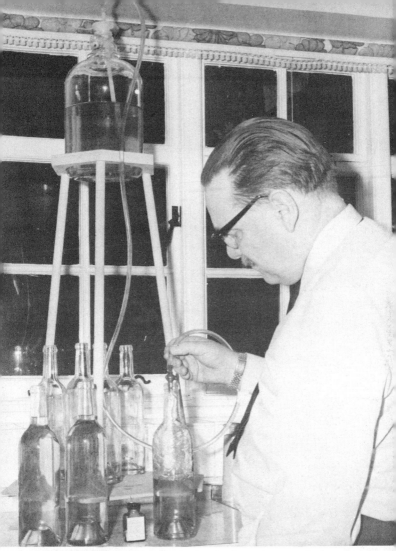

BOTTLING SESSION: All the bottles have been washed and sterilised, and the wine is now siphoned into them, leaving about ¾" air space below the bottom of the cork. A small, positive tap (as illustrated) is a great help in controlling the flow—and avoiding a mess.

Corking, capsuling and labelling. Use a corking gun and small mallet to drive corks home, then fit an attractive capsule and label worthy of your wine.

BELOW: Useful racks for wine storage. It is easy to make your own.

ABOVE: Seyve Villard grapes growing on the wall of the author's house.

BELOW: A typical display by a Winemaking Circle.

ABOVE: Judging in progress at a large competition.

BELOW: Winemakers enjoy many happy social occasions such as this barbecue.

If using a hydrometer, test the juice and determine how much sugar has to be added; dissolve it in the juice, and pour the juice into your fermenting vessel. (Many winemakers prefer to add only half the sugar at this stage and the remainder two or three days later.)

You can then either (*a*) rely upon the natural yeast (the bloom upon the grapes, of which sufficient will have passed into the juice to start fermentation) or, preferably (*b*) add one Campden tablet per gallon, and, 24 hours later, a vigorous yeast starter of your own choice. A good yeast nutrient will also help.

Fermentation, in a warm place, will be more rapid than with the usual run of country wines but the advent of chillier weather will slow it down.

If you are not using a hydrometer, of course, add your initial 8 oz. of sugar, and thereafter keep a close eye on your ferment, for it is likely to require further sugar almost every day, although the ferment and sugar consumption will be slower in the latter stages than in the early one.

Thereafter the process is the same as with any country wine.

RED WINE

If using a hydrometer, press a few of the grapes to determine the specific gravity of the juice and how much sugar to add. (If not using a hydrometer, it is best to add at least 1¼ lb.)

Remove the stalks of the grapes: place the grapes in a tub or large crock (a cylindrical one is convenient) and crush them by hand or with a piece of hardwood and, if using the natural yeast, add the sugar and yeast nutrient, stirring very thoroughly. If using a special yeast add one Campden tablet per gallon, and 24 hours later stir in the sugar and add the yeast.

Use a disc of heavy hardwood (oak or beech) fitting very loosely in the cylindrical crock, to hold the skins down below the surface of the liquid. Bore holes in it with a 2 in. bit. Each day push this "sinker" down to keep the skins wet.

September

This is important or you may get poor colour extraction and the "cap" of skins may acetify. Keep the crock in a warm place for up to 10 days, according to the depth of colour you require, but not more, then strain off the liquor into your fermenting vessel and add (by stages if not using a hydrometer) the balance of the sugar. If you can, press the "pulp" to get "just that little extra".

Keep this wine, of course, in an opaque or coloured fermenter to preserve its colour, and thereafter continue as for any ordinary country wine.

MEAD
(by S. H. Pullinger, Alresford)

Take 3–4½ lb. of mild honey, amount according to dryness or sweetness of wine required. If a wine yeast is to be used, have it activated and ready in advance.

Bring the honey to the boil in two or three times its volume of water. Stir with wooden spoon until honey is dissolved, or it may burn. Skim off any scum which rises.

To the hot liquid add approximately ½ oz. of citric acid and the yeast nutrient. Alternatively, one may use the juice of 4–6 lemons, when only half the yeast nutrient need be added.

Add the rest of the water when convenient, transfer to fermenting containers and add yeast when cool. A narrow neck and air-lock are advisable. Since there is a gallon of water and several pounds of honey there will be about nine to 10 pints of liquid. This will allow for a full gallon after racking, which should take place when the wine is beginning to clear and a definite layer of sludge can be seen at the bottom. Wine made now would be worth drinking at Christmas but would be better for keeping.

MELOMEL
(Rosehip Mead)

If you wish to use rose hips for flavouring to make **Melomel,** as a fruit flavoured mead is called, use about 4 lb. Boil them in a gallon of water for five or 10 minutes, and when

128

cool mash them with your hands or a piece of hardwood, and strain through butter muslin.

To this add 4 lb. honey, the juice of 2 lemons, and yeast nutrient, and stir until the honey is dissolved. When lukewarm add the yeast and ferment as usual. It is an improvement for this mead to use a sherry yeast and ferment in the sherry manner, i.e., **after the first racking** (not before) have your fermenting container only $\frac{7}{8}$ full, and use an empty air-lock, the end of which can be lightly plugged with a small piece of cotton-wool, thus exposing the mead to air but preventing the entrance of any vinegar flies, allowing a degree of oxidisation. But you can also use an ordinary wine yeast and ferment and mature throughout in the usual way if you wish.

To make **Metheglin** use 4 lb. honey, 1 oz. hops, and $\frac{1}{2}$ oz. root ginger to the gallon, or with the same amount of honey and water, 2 cloves and $\frac{1}{4}$ oz. cinnamon bark, or $\frac{1}{8}$ oz. of carraway seeds.

Marjoram, balm, mace, lemon and orange peel, and cinnamon, are also flavourings which can be tried, but it is as well not to overdo them.

BLACKBERRY WINE

	British	Metric	U.S.A.
Blackberries	4 lb.	1¾ kilos	3 lb.
Sugar	3 lb.	1½ kilos	2¼ lb.
Water	1 gallon	4½ litres	1 gallon

Yeast & nutrient; pectic enzyme

The fruit should be picked when ripe and dry, on a sunny day. Wash it well, being careful to remove any of the small maggots sometimes found in blackberries. Place the fruit in a crock, and crush it with a wooden spoon. Pour over it the gallon of boiling water. Stir well, allow to become lukewarm (about 70°F., 21°C.), then add the pectic enzyme according to instructions, and a day later the yeast and nutrient. Cover closely and leave for four or five days, stirring daily. Strain through some nylon netting or a nylon sieve on to 3 lb. of granulated sugar. Stir well to make sure that all is dissolved. Pour into dark fermenting jar, filling to shoulder, and fit air-lock. Keep the spare liquor in a smaller

September

bottle also fitted with a trap or plug of cotton-wool. When the ferment quietens sufficiently for there to be no risk of it foaming through the trap (after, say, a week) top up with the spare wine to the base of the neck and refit trap. Leave until it clears and then rack for the first time.

DEWBERRY, LOGANBERRY AND RASPBERRY WINES

. . . can be made to exactly the same recipe as Blackberry Wine.

MEDLAR WINE

	British	Metric	U.S.A.
Medlars	6 lb.	2¾ kilos	5 lb.
Sugar	3 lb.	1½ kilos	2¼ lb.
Grape tannin	½ teasp.	½ teasp.	½ teasp.
Water	1 gallon	4½ litres	1 gallon
Yeast & nutrient; pectic enzyme			

Chop the fruit and pour over it two quarts boiling water; stir in 1½ lb. sugar, and 1 quart cold water. Leave till cool, then add ingredients. Cover closely and leave in warm place. After three days strain into fermenting jar and top up to bottom of neck with cold water. Fit air-lock and continue as usual.

CIDER OR PERRY

Cider is made from apples, perry from pears.

Strictly speaking, only natural sugar of the fruit should be employed and no sugar should be added.

A press or juice extractor is essential. Put the fruit in a tub or polythene dustbin and crush it with a "masher", a heavy balk of timber. Then express the juice by means of a press or by wrapping the fruit a little at a time in a stout cloth and twisting or pressing it. Collect the juice in a jar, stand it on a tray in a warm place (about 70°F., 21°C.) and add yeast. Invert a small glass over the top of the jar. For a few days the jar will froth over and must be kept topped up, but when the ferment quietens fit air-lock and proceed as for any other wine.

130

September

SPARKLING MEAD

	British	Metric	U.S.A.
Honey	3 lb.	1½ kilos	2¼ lb.
Citric acid	1 tablesp.	1 tablesp.	2 tablesps.
Water	1 gallon	4½ litres	1 gallon
Maury or wine yeast and nutrient			

Bring the water to the boil for a minute or so, and then allow it to cool to 120°F. (50°C.) Warm up the honey meantime to the same temperature, and then mix the two, stirring well to dissolve the honey.

Allow the honey liquor to cool to 70°F. (21°C.) and then add the acid, a good yeast nutrient and the prepared yeast culture. Failing this, one can use a level teaspoonful of granulated yeast, but there is then a risk if racking should happen to be delayed later on, of spoiling the delicate mead flavour. Pour the liquor into a fermenting jar, filling it to the bottom of the neck, and keep the surplus in a covered jug nearby. Put both vessels in a warm place (65–70°F., 17–21°C.). As the fermentation froths out of the jar, as it may do, top up from the jug. When the vigorous ferment slows down, and froth ceases to form, fill the jar to the bottom of the neck, fit an air-lock, and clean the exterior. When fermentation stops completely move the jar to a cold room and leave it there for a fortnight or three weeks before siphoning the mead off the lees, and into a clean jar. Use a well-fitting waxed cork but do not wire it down. The following March (after roughly six months' storage) siphon the mead off the lees again and to the gallon add 2 oz. honey (or white sugar) dissolved in ¼ pint of water, boiled and cooled as before. Mix thoroughly and bottle, using strong bottles (of champagne type, if possible), cork, and wire or tie the corks down.

Note that honey is usually deficient in trace minerals and is sometimes difficult to ferment. It is therefore important to use a yeast nutrient.

September

MULBERRY WINE

	British	Metric	U.S.A.
Mulberries	3½ lb.	1½ kilos	2½ lb.
Raisins	1 lb.	½ kilo	1 lb.
or Concentrate (red)	½ pint	280 mls.	½ pint
Sugar	2½ lb.	1¼ kilos	2 lb.
Campden tablet	1	1	1
Water	1 gallon	4½ litres	1 gallon
Yeast & nutrient; pectic enzyme			

Wash the mulberries, having removed the stalks, and chop and mince the raisins. If using concentrate, pour that into the vessel. Pour on the boiling water; when cool add crushed Campden tablet, half the sugar, the nutrient, and the yeast. Stir well. Ferment for four days on "pulp", then strain, add remaining sugar, and ferment, rack and bottle in the usual way. A Bordeaux yeast is preferable.

PEAR WINE

	British	Metric	U.S.A.
Pears	5 lb.	2¼ kilos	4 lb.
Sugar	3 lb.	1½ kilos	2¼ lb.
Lemons	2	2	2
Water	1 gallon	4½ litres	1 gallon
Yeast & nutrient			

Really ripe pears, even "sleepy" ones, are best for your purpose. Do not bother to peel or core them, but chop them, being careful to save any juice, put them into a large saucepan, and add the water and any juice. Bring slowly to the boil, and simmer gently for not more than 20 minutes, or the wine may not clear later. Strain the liquor off into a large crock on to the sugar, and add the juice of the two lemons to supply some acid, and yeast nutrient, since pears are deficient in both. When the liquor has cooled to blood heat transfer to a fermenting jar, add a wine yeast or a level teaspoonful of granulated yeast, and fit air-lock, for contact with air is not only risky because of possible infection, but also because it may cause oxidation.

Do not fill the jar to the bottom of the neck but keep a little of the liquor aside in a closely covered jug or another

air-locked bottle, to be added when the first vigorous fermentation has quietened and there is no longer risk of the wine
foaming out through the air-lock. An excellent wine can be
made in this way, but if you have a fondness for dry wine,
for which pears are particularly suitable, cut the sugar down
until the original gravity of the liquor is about 1090, or 2 lb.
3 ozs. per gallon.

ROSE HIP WINE

	British	Metric	U.S.A.
Fresh rose hips	2 lb.	1 kilo	1½ lb.
or			
Dried rose hips	½ lb.	¼ kilo	½ lb.
Citric acid	1 teasp.	1 teasp.	1 teasp.
Sugar	3 lb.	1½ kilos	2¼ lb.
Water	1 gallon	4½ litres	1 gallon
Yeast & nutrient; pectic enzyme			

The best time to gather your rose hips, of which there
are usually plenty in the hedgerows, is immediately after the
first frost. Wash them well, and then cut them in half or
crush them with a piece of wood or mallet. (This is unnecessary with the dried rose hips). Put the sugar into a crock,
then the crushed rose hips, and pour over them the boiling
water. Stir well to dissolve the sugar. When the liquor has
cooled sufficiently for you to be able to put your finger in
it comfortably, add yeast (a general purpose wine yeast, or
a level teaspoon of granulated yeast), acid, enzyme, and
nutrient. Leave in a warm place, cover closely for a fortnight,
and stir daily. Then strain through a jelly bag, a sieve, or
some nylon netting into a fermentation jar and fit air-lock
When the wine clears (after about three months) siphon
into a fresh jar, and leave for a further three months before
racking again and bottling. Since the only main ingredient
which has to be bought is the sugar, this is a most economical
wine to make, and I am told that the hips contain a high
proportion of Vitamin C, so it is probably beneficial as well!

Rosehip Syrup provides an easy way of making wine
too. And a 6 oz. or 8 oz. bottle is sufficient to make a gallon.

Brands commonly available are Delrosa (in 6 oz. and
12 oz. bottles), Hipsy (in 8 oz.) and Optrose (6 oz. and 12 oz.).

October

Merely bring the water to the boil, add the syrup and sugar, and stir well to dissolve. Cool to 70°F. (21°C.), and add the yeast and nutrient. Pour into fermenting jar and fit air-lock. Leave in a warm place. After a week top up to bottom of neck with cold boiled water and refit lock. Ferment, rack and bottle in the usual way.

ROSEHIP PUREE

as can sometimes be purchased, also makes excellent wine using 1 or 2 lb. to the gallon.

ROWANBERRY WINE

	British	Metric	U.S.A.
Rowanberries	3 lb.	1½ kilos	2¼ lb.
Raisins	1 lb.	½ kilo	¾ lb.
or Concentrate (red)	½ pint	280 mls.	½ pint
Wheat	½ lb.	¼ kilo	½ lb.
Sugar	3 lb.	1½ kilos	2¼ lb.
Water	1 gallon	4½ litres	1 gallon
Citric acid	1 tablesp.	1 tablesp.	2 tablesps.
Yeast & nutrient			

Pour the boiling water over the berries and let it stand four days, then strain. Put in the sugar, chopped raisins (or concentrate), acid, and wheat and stir until the sugar is dissolved, then add the yeast and nutrient. Leave to ferment 16 days, closely covered, then strain into fermenting jar and fit air-lock. When it clears, siphon into bottles, corking lightly at first.

RED TABLE WINE

	British	Metric	U.S.A.
Elderberries	10 lb.	4½ kilos	8 lb.
Raisins	10 lb.	4½ kilos	8 lb.
or Concentrate (red)	5 pints	2½ litres	5 pints
Sugar	4 lb.	2 kilos	3 lb.
Water	4½ gallons	18 litres	4½ gallons
Beaujolais yeast & nutrient			

Crush the elderberries and strain off the juice. Leach the "pulp" by adding 1 gallon of boiling water, stirring for 5 minutes and then straining off the "pulp". Repeat this treatment with a second gallon of boiling water. Add the raisins (or concentrate), and nutrients to this elderberry extract followed by another 1½ gallons of water. When cool add the yeast starter and ferment on the "pulp" for four days. Strain off the "pulp" and press lightly. Add the sugar, stir until completely dissolved and make up the volume to 4½ gallons with water. thereafter continue as usual with fermenting, racking and bottling.

HAWTHORNBERRY WINE

	British	Metric	U.S.A.
Hawthornberries	½ gallon	2¼ litres	½ gallon
White grape juice concentrate	½ pint	280 mls.	½ pint
Sugar	2½ lb.	1¼ kilos	2 lb.
Pectolase	1 teasp.	5 mls.	1 teasp.
Citric acid	1 tablesp.	15 gms.	2 tablesps.
Water	1 gallon	4½ litres	1 gallon
1 Campden tablet; yeast & nutrient			

Rinse the berries to remove dust and "foreign bodies". Measure out four pints of them and pour over them six pints of boiling water. Leave to cool, then crush them with a stainless steel spoon (or your hands) and stir in the Pectolase, crushed Campden tablet, and acid. Twenty-four hours later add the concentrated grape juice, sugar, yeast and nutrient. Keep covered in a warm place for five days, then strain into a one-gallon jar, top up with water to base of neck, fit trap, and continue as usual.

BILBERRY WINE

	British	Metric	U.S.A.
Fresh bilberries	3 lb.	1½ kilos	3 lb.
Sugar	3 lb.	1½ kilos	2¼ lb.
Citric acid	1 dessertsp.	2 teasps.	1 tablesp.
Water	1 gallon	4½ litres	1 gallon
Yeast & nutrient			

Pour half the water, boiling, over the bilberries, and stir in the sugar, and, when the liquor has cooled, add the remaining water (cold), the acid, nutrient and yeast. Cover and ferment on the pulp for four or five days before straining into a jar and fitting air-lock. Thereafter proceed as usual.

November

CRANBERRY WINE
. . . can be made to the same recipe.

SUGAR BEET WINE

	British	Metric	U.S.A.
Sugar beet	4½ lb.	2 kilos	3 lb.
Sugar	2 lb. 2 ozs.	1 kilo	1½ lb.
Bruised ginger	1 oz.	25 gms.	1 oz.
Water	9 pints	4½ litres	9 pints
Yeast & nutrient			

This is a recipe devised many years ago by Cdr. I. Mudie, of Chilbolton, and it made a sturdy, dry wine of 15.4 per cent alcohol by volume.

Wash or scrub the beet, slice them and boil with the ginger in 7 pints of the water for 1½ hours. Then strain on to the remaining 1½ pints of cold water. If you wish you can press the beet (as I did) thus obtaining an extra half-pint of liquor. To this add 2 lb. 2 ozs. of sugar and boil in for three-quarters of an hour. Make up to 1 gallon if necessary, allow to cool until tepid, then pour into fermenting jar, add yeast and nutrient, and fit air-lock. Leave for three months, then siphon into fresh jars or bottles. A warming wine for winter nights!

APRICOT WINE

	British	Metric	U.S.A.
Dried apricots	2 lb.	1 kilo	1½ lb.
Wheat	1 lb.	½ kilo	¾ lb.
Sugar	3 lb.	1½ kilos	2¼ lb.
Lemons, juice	2	2	2
Grape tannin	1 teasp.	1 teasp.	1 teasp.
Water	1 gallon	4½ litres	1 gallon
Yeast & nutrient; pectic enzyme			

Cut up the apricots, put into one gallon of water, and bring to the boil; simmer for half-an-hour, then strain (without pressing). Add the other ingredients to the liquor and, when cool enough, the yeast, and enzyme; ferment for three weeks, closely covered, in a warm place, stir daily. Strain into a fermenting bottle, make up with cold water to one gallon, fit air-lock, and ferment for a further month. Then strain, bottle, and cork tightly.

November

CELERY WINE

	British	Metric	U.S.A.
Celery (green and white)	4 lb.	2 kilos	3 lb.
Sugar	3 lb.	1½ kilos	2¼ lb.
Citric acid	1 tablesp.	1 tablesp.	2 tablesps.
Water	1 gallon	4½ litres	1 gallon
Yeast & nutrient			

Chop up the celery into short lengths and boil it in the water until it is tender to extract the flavour. Strain (if you like you can use the cooked celery as a vegetable) and stir in sugar and acid. If you require wine of a golden colour use Demerara instead of white. Then, when you are sure all the sugar has dissolved, allow the liquor to cool to 70°F. (21°C.) before adding the yeast (a G.P. wine yeast or a level teaspoon of granulated yeast) and yeast nutrient. Keep in a crock or bowl, closely covered, in a warm place for four days, then stir well, transfer to fermenting jar, fit air-lock. Leave until it clears, then siphon off the lees. Leave until fermentation has completely finished, there is a firm sediment, and wine is really clear, before siphoning into clean bottles as usual. The slight bitterness of this wine makes it an excellent aperitif.

CLOVE WINE

	British	Metric	U.S.A.
Cloves	1 oz.	30 gms.	1 oz.
Brown sugar	3 lb.	1½ kilos	2¼ lb.
Ginger	1 oz.	30 gms.	1 oz.
Lemons	3	3	3
Seville orange	1	1	1
Water	1 gallon	4½ litres	1 gallon
Yeast & nutrient			

Grate the peel from the orange and lemons, avoiding the white pith, and put it in a small muslin bag with the cloves and bruised ginger. Bring the water to the boil, drop in the bag and simmer gently for an hour. Then take out the bag, place the sugar in a crock, and pour boiling water over it. Stir to dissolve the sugar, and add the yeast nutrient. Allow to cool to 70°F. (21°C.) then add the yeast, a wine

137

November

yeast or one level teaspoonful of granulated yeast. Leave closely covered for four days in a warm place, then stir, pour into fermenting jar, and fit air-lock. Leave till it clears, then siphon off for the first time into fresh jar and refit air-lock. When the wine has cleared completely, has thrown a second deposit, and all fermentation has ceased, bottle.

CORNMEAL WINE
(or "Golden Dinamite")

Since many home winemakers now seem to be using Messrs. Hidalgo's concentrates, they may care to try this recipe which the firm has evolved.

	British	Metric	U.S.A.
Yellow cornmeal or cornflour	2 lb.	1 kilo	1½ lb.
Sugar	3 lb.	1½ kilos	2¼ lb.
Lemons, juice	2	2	2
Oranges, juice	3	3	3
Grape juice concentrate	3 pints	1¾ litres	3 pints
Tartaric acid	1 oz.	30 gms.	1 oz.
Ammonium phosphate	¼ oz.	10 gms.	¼ oz.
Ground rice	¼ oz.	10 gms.	¼ oz.
Campden tablets	2	2	2
Water	2 gallons	9 litres	2 gallons
Yeast			

Mix all the ingredients together, then add Hidalgo yeast (supplied free with the concentrate) and set aside in a warm place (65–70°F., 17–21°C) to ferment, closely covered, for at least 30 days, stirring once a day. Siphon off and 30 days later rack off again; it will then be ready to drink.

HOP WINE

	British	Metric	U.S.A.
Hops	3 ozs.	75 gms.	3 ozs.
Ginger (bruised)	1 oz.	25 gms	1 oz.
Sugar	3 lb.	1½ kilos	2¼ lb.
Orange	1	1	1
Lemon	1	1	1
Water	1 gallon	4½ litres	1 gallon
Yeast & nutrient			

138

Boil the hops and ginger in the water for one hour, then strain and pour the liquor over the sugar and orange and lemon juice. Put all into a fermenting jar with wine yeast or a level teaspoonful of granulated yeast and fit air-lock. When it has fermented right out add ½ lb. of chopped raisins and ½ lb. of loaf sugar and bung tightly. Leave for six months before bottling.

PARSNIP SHERRY (Light)

	British	Metric	U.S.A.
Young parsnips	4 lb.	2 kilos	3 lb.
Sugar	2½ lb.	1¼ kilos	2 lb.
Malt extract	2 tablesps.	2 tablesps.	4 tablesps.
Citric acid	1 teasp.	1 teasp.	1 teasp.
Water	1 gallon	4½ litres	1 gallon
Yeast			

Scrub the parsnips (which are best lifted after the first frost) but do not peel. Cut into chunks or slices and boil gently in the water until tender, than strain. Stir in the malt, acid and sugar, and when cool add the yeast. Ferment, closely covered, in a warm place for 10 days, then put into a fermenting bottle and fit air-lock. Siphon it off, and bottle when all fermentation has ceased and wine has cleared.

QUINCE WINE

	British	Metric	U.S.A.
Quinces	20	20	20
Sugar	2 lb.	1½ kilos	2¼ lb.
Lemons	2	2	2
Water	1 gallon	4½ litres	1 gallon
Yeast & nutrient			

Grate the quinces as near to the core as possible, and boil the "pulp" in the water for 15 minutes (not more, or the wine may not clear subsequently). Strain on to the sugar and add the juice and grated rinds of the two lemons. Allow the liquor to cool before adding the yeast (a wine yeast or a level teaspoonful of granulated yeast). Leave it to stand for 48 hours, closely covered, in a warm place, then strain into fermenting bottle and fit air-lock. Siphon off for the

December

first time when it clears. This wine has a strong individualistic bouquet, but sometimes ferments for an extraordinarily long time, so extra-careful attention to racking is necessary to stabilise it, with the addition of one Campden tablet per gallon finally.

SULTANA SHERRY

	British	Metric	U.S.A.
Sultanas or "white raisins"	1 lb.	$\frac{1}{2}$ kilo	$\frac{3}{4}$ lb.
Grapes	1 lb.	$\frac{1}{2}$ kilo	$\frac{3}{4}$ lb.
Barley	$\frac{1}{2}$ lb.	$\frac{1}{4}$ kilo	$\frac{1}{2}$ lb.
Sugar	$2\frac{1}{2}$ lb.	$1\frac{1}{4}$ kilos	2 lb.
Citric acid	$\frac{1}{2}$ teasp.	$\frac{1}{2}$ teasp.	$\frac{1}{2}$ teasp.
Water	1 gallon	$4\frac{1}{2}$ litres	1 gallon
Sherry yeast & nutrient			

Soak the barley overnight in half a pint of (extra) water and the next day mince both grain and sultanas. Bring water to the boil and pour it over the grain and fruit, then crush the grapes manually and add. Stir in the sugar and make sure it is all dissolved. Allow to cool just tepid, then introduce the nutrient, acid and yeast. Ferment closely covered for 10 days, stirring vigorously daily, then strain into fermenting jar and fit air-lock.

SLOE WINE

	British	Metric	U.S.A.
Sloes	3 lb.	$1\frac{1}{2}$ kilos	$2\frac{1}{4}$ lb.
Raisins	$\frac{1}{2}$ lb.	$\frac{1}{4}$ kilo	$\frac{1}{2}$ lb.
or Concentrate (red)	$\frac{1}{4}$ pint	140 mls.	$\frac{1}{4}$ pint
Sugar	3 lb.	$1\frac{1}{2}$ kilos	$2\frac{1}{2}$ lb.
Water	6 pints	$3\frac{1}{2}$ litres	6 pints
Yeast & nutrient; pectic enzyme			

Place the sloes in a crock or bowl and pour over them the boiling water. Mash the sloes well, adding the minced raisins or concentrate, and, when cool, the pectic enzyme, followed 24 hours later by the yeast and nutrient, 2 lb. sugar and, of course, the yeast. Stir well, cover with a cloth and ferment in a warm room for 10 days, stirring each day. Then

140

strain, add remaining sugar, and pour into fermenting jar. Fit air-lock and leave in a warm room for four weeks to ferment, then taste. If too bitter, a little more sugar can be added. Refit air-lock and store in a cool place to clear for a few weeks. When clear, bottle and store for at least a year before use.

SLOE GIN

Half-fill a 2 lb. clean Kilner jar with pricked clean sloes, adding 4 oz. of castor sugar, and fill the jar up to the top with dry gin.

Place a ring on the top, also the lid, and screw down tightly. Shake the jar daily until the sugar is dissolved and the liquid has taken on a dark colour. ¼ oz. of almond essence can be added after two weeks.

Leave the sloes in the jar for two months in all, shaking up fairly often. When the gin is to be bottled, preferably into a half-size liqueur bottle, the liquid must be run through doubled muslin several times to ensure all particles which would otherwise mar the clarity are kept from the bottle.

BEETROOT WINE

	British	Metric	U.S.A.
Beetroot	3 lb.	1½ kilos	2¼ lb.
Sugar	3 lb.	1½ kilos	2¼ lb.
Cloves	6	6	6
Lemon, juice	1	1	1
Ginger, bruised	1 oz.	25 gms.	1 oz.
Water	1 gallon	4½ litres	1 gallon
Yeast & nutrient			

Wash the beetroot well, but do not peel; cut them up and boil them in some of the water until tender but not mushy. Strain on to the sugar, lemon juice, spices, and the rest of the water, and stir until the sugar is dissolved. When the liquor is cool stir in the yeast, then cover closely, and leave in a warm place, giving it a stir each day. After three days strain the liquor through nylon into an opaque fermenting jar or bottle, and fit air-lock. When it clears siphon it into dark bottles. (Test it by lifting some out in a glass

December

tube: insert the glass tube in the wine, but not as far as the yeast sediment, press the tip of your forefinger over the top end and you will be able to lift out a "column" of wine clearly showing its condition at various depths). It is important that opaque jars or dark bottles should be used, otherwise on exposure to the light beetroot wine will lose the glorious colour which is its principal feature and turn an unattractive brown. If you have only clear glass vessels, wrap them in brown paper, invert sugar bags over them, or keep them in a dark cupboard.

GINGER WINE

	British	Metric	U.S.A.
Root ginger	3 ozs.	75 gms.	3 ozs.
Sultanas	1 lb.	½ kilo	¾ lb.
or Concentrate (white)	½ pint	280 mls.	½ pint
Sugar	2½ lb.	1¼ kilos	2 lb.
Bananas (no skins)	2 lb.	1 kilo	1½ lb.
Water	1 gallon	4½ litres	1 gallon
All purpose yeast & nutrient			

Break the root ginger into pieces, mince sultanas and put them (or the concentrate) into a plastic bucket with the sugar. Pour on five pints of boiling water. Meanwhile chop the bananas into small pieces and boil them in one pint of water until they go mushy, then strain the banana liquid into the bucket, stirring well to dissolve the sugar.

Ferment in a covered bucket for 10 days, stirring twice daily, then strain into a gallon jar. Fit air-lock and leave to ferment. Rack three months later, by then the wine should have stopped fermenting if it has been kept in a warm place. Rack again about three months later. If made this month the wine will be ready for next Christmas—if you manage to keep it that long! Green colouring can be added if one wishes to give some authenticity, then you *will* baffle your friends.

December

MIXED DRIED FRUIT WINE

This is a glorious, golden wine which is simplicity itself to make.

	British	Metric	U.S.A.
Dried fruit in cartons	3 12 oz. cartons	1 kilo	2 lb.
Wheat	1 lb.	½ kilo	¾ lb.
Sugar	3 lb.	1½ kilos	2¼ lb.
Citric acid	1 tablesp.	1 talbesp.	2 tablesps.
Water	1 gallon	4½ litres	1 gallon
Yeast & nutrient			

Make up a starter bottle two days or so before you need it with half a pint of orange juice—it can be a little diluted to make up the quantity—1 oz. of sugar, a little yeast nutrient and the general-purpose wine yeast. Place it in a temperature of about 70°F. (21°C.).

You can obtain your 12 oz. cartons of fruit (sultanas, raisins and currants) from Woolworths. Tip all the fruit, grain and sugar into a crock, and pour over them the boiling water, stirring to dissolve the sugar. When cool add the contents of the starter bottle and ¼ oz. citric acid, and stir well in. Cover closely and leave in a warm place (65–70°F., 17–21°C.) for three weeks, stirring vigorously daily. Then strain into fermenting bottle and fit air-lock, and rack off for the first time when it clears. This wine can be drunk after six months and it is doubly useful in that it can be made at any time of the year.

PARSNIP WINE

	British	Metric	U.S.A.
Parsnips	7 lb.	3 kilos	5½ lb.
Lemons	2	2	2
Water	2½ gallons	11 litres	2½ gallons
Yeast & nutrient			

Scrub and scrape the parsnips; then slice them and boil them in the water until tender, but not mushy, or the wine will not clear later, The parsnips can be boiled in half the water, if necessary, and the remaining water added afterwards, warm.

December

Then strain through a coarse cloth tied over a crock, but do not hurry the process or press the parsnips in any way, for again this may be fatal to the wine's clarity. A thorough, slow, unforced straining is essential. Measure the liquor, add 3 lb. white sugar to a gallon, and finally the juice of the two lemons. Bring to the boil and simmer for three-quarters of an hour. Turn into crock, and when liquor has cooled to 70°F. (21°C.) add yeast and yeast nutrient. Cover closely with a thick cloth and allow to remain in a warm place for ten days, stirring well from the bottom each day. Then strain into fermenting jar or cask, fit air-lock, and leave for about six months in a cooler place; it should then be clearing. Siphon it off the lees, bottle, and keep six months longer.

Many people have difficulty in clearing parsnip wine, but if you follow these instructions carefully yours will be of brilliant clarity and excellent colour.

SARSAPARILLA WINE

	British	Metric	U.S.A.
Sarsaparilla	1½ ozs.	35 gms.	1½ ozs.
Caramel	¾ oz.	25 gms.	½ oz.
Sugar	3 lb.	1½ kilos	2¼ lb.
Tartaric acid	1½ ozs.	35 gms.	1 oz.
Water	1 gallon	4½ litres	1 gallon
Yeast & nutrient			

Infuse sarsaparilla and caramel in 1½ pints boiling water, and add sugar. Allow to cool, add 6½ pints cold water, acid, nutrient and yeast. Ferment, rack and bottle in usual way.

WHEAT WINE

	British	Metric	U.S.A.
Wheat	1 lb.	½ kilo	¾ lb.
Brown sugar	3½ lb.	1½ kilos	2¼ lb.
Raisins	2 lb.	1 kilo	1½ lb.
or Concentrate (white)	1 pint	560 mls.	1 pint
Potatoes (large)	2	2	2
Lemons	2	2	2
Water	1 gallon	4½ litres	1 gallon
Yeast & nutrient			

December

Soak the wheat in one pint of the water overnight to soften it. Wash (or peel if old) the potatoes, and slice; put the wheat and raisins through a mincer. Put sugar, wheat, potatoes and raisins (or concentrate) in a bowl and pour on hot (not necessarily boiling) water. Add the juice of the two lemons, and allow to cool to 70°F. (21°C.). Add yeast, and yeast nutrient. Cover well with cloth and allow to stand for 10 days, **stirring well daily**. Strain, put into fermenting bottle, and fit air-lock. Siphon off into bottles when clear and no longer fermenting.

CHRISTLETON
(by Dr. L. W. F. Rowe)

If you, like me, are both mean and lazy, try this recipe! "Mean and lazy" because it will give you a wine which is both cheap and very easy to make, and drinkable within a couple of months of being started. It's "a light dry red wine equally suitable for Sunday dinner or for lazing in the garden on a hot sunny day" . . . need I say more?

	British	Metric	U.S.A.
Dried elderberries	4¼ ozs.	125 gms.	4 oz.
Sugar (or glucose)	2 lb.	1 kilo	1¾ lb.
Dry cider	1¼ pints	700 mls.	1¼ pints
Citric acid	1 dessertsp.	2 teasps.	1 tablesp.
Water	1 gallon	4½ litres	1 gallon
Wine yeast & nutrient; pectolase; 3 3 mgm. Vit. B. tablets			

Place the dried elderberries in a saucepan with enough water to cover them comfortably. Bring to the boil and simmer for 15 minutes. Strain off the juice, pressing lightly, and return the berries to the pan. Add just enough water to cover, bring to the boil again and simmer for 10 minutes. Strain again and repeat this process, simmering for 10 minutes at a time, until just about all the colour has gone out of the berries. Stir the sugar, citric acid and yeast nutrient, into the hot liquid and put aside to cool. When down to about 80°F. (32°C.), add the cider, pectolase and yeast starter (and Vitamin B₁ tablets) and ferment out in the usual way.

Christmas Drinks

ANGELICA LIQUEUR

And here is a recipe for a Christmas luxury, by Mrs. Betty Parker, of Whitchurch, Hants.:

1 oz. Angelica stem	1 pint brandy
1 oz. boiled bitter almonds	1 pint syrup made with white sugar

Steep the angelica and almonds in the brandy for a week, then strain off and add the syrup to the liquor. "Improves with keeping—if you can keep it!"

CHRISTMAS GLOW

1 bottle of one of your red wines	1 cup granulated sugar
1 small glass cherry brandy	2 ozs. honey
1 glass brandy	Grated nutmeg to taste
1 sliced lemon	About ½ pint boiling water

Heat wine, honey, lemon, nutmeg, sugar to near boiling point; then add brandy and cherry brandy and lastly the water. Serve immediately.

CHRISTMAS PUNCH

For those who like punches (and who doesn't at Christmas?) here is an excellent recipe:

Rub eight pieces of lump sugar on two big lemons, collecting all the fragrant essential oil possible. Put the lumps in a bright sauce pan with ¼ teaspoon of ground cinnamon, ¼ teaspoon of grated nutmeg and ground cloves mixed, and a fair pinch of salt. Put in 8 oz. each of brandy and Jamaica rum and add 16 oz. of boiling water. Heat up the bowl, and strain into it the juice of two lemons. Heat up the mixture in the pan just to miss boiling point and strain it through muslin in colander or sieve into the bowl. Now add one pint of a good white country wine—elderflower gooseberry, rhubarb or apple, preferably sparkling—and serve with a cube of pineapple in each cup.

COOMASSIE

In a small tumbler break the yolk of a fresh egg and mix in one teaspoon icing sugar. Add six drops Angostura, 1½ oz. sherry and half that amount of brandy. Fill glass with shaved ice, shake well and strain. Dust with fresh-grated nutmeg and powdered cinnamon. This approaches a flip.

ADVOCAAT

Whatever you do, do not fail to make this gorgeous advocaat. We can guarantee that this recipe (for which we are indebted to Mr. G. Wilson, of Ryde, I.O.W.) will produce a liqueur of authentic colour and consistency, smooth, creamy and wholly delightful.

4 yolks from medium-size eggs
7 fl. ozs. cheap brandy
¾ large tin Ideal milk (the one equivalent to 1¾ pints of milk)
4 ozs. sugar syrup (2 lb. to 1 pint
1 teaspoon Vanilla essence
½ teaspoon saffron yellow food colouring

Put all the ingredients with the exception of the brandy into a liquidiser, and liquidise for 20 seconds. Then pour into the top half of a *double* saucepan with a lid.

Put water in the lower saucepan and boil for about an hour, until the mixture in the upper pan thickens and looks similar to a cooled jelly (when the pan is jerked sideways sharply the mixture will come away from the side and then flop back again). Check that the lower pan does not boil dry.

Leave the mixture to cool, then put into the liquidiser with the brandy for 30 seconds.

If too thick liquidise with some of the remaining Ideal milk. Bottle and leave in a cool place for 24 hours.

ADVOCAAT (2)
(By Mr. Halls of Kings Lynn, Norfolk)

Six fresh free range eggs. Whisk the whites with a little sugar and then add yolks. Add 1 tin of NESTLES condensed milk and whisk again (tin equivalent to 1⅝ pints fresh milk).

Add 1 pocket size or quarter size brandy and whisk again. Then add about 1¼ pints of wheat or barley wine and whisk again. Taste result. Shake well before drinking.

147

ORANGE COCKTAIL

Mix: 1 bottle orange wine, 1 wineglass whisky, and a dash of rum.

HOT COFFEE RUM

This is an excellent after-dinner drink for which, if possible, the coffee should be freshly ground, as well as freshly made.

Into a small saucepan put six lumps of sugar, the finely pared rind of two oranges, six cloves, and a stick of cinnamon. Add enough rum to cover the sugar and bring nearly to the boil, stirring gently until the sugar is dissolved. Take care that it does not catch fire.

When ready stir the mixture into six cups of very strong very hot black coffee and serve immediately.

MILK PUNCH
(Modern version of an 1835 recipe)

1 quart fresh milk
1 bottle rum or brandy
1 pint rum (if desired)
1 gallon water

6 seville oranges (or six ordinary oranges and six lemons)
3½ lb. sugar

Peel the fruit very thinly, or use a grater to exclude all white pith, which has a bitter taste, and squeeze out all the juice. Soak the peel in the spirits for four days in a corked large bottle. Put the sugar in a bowl and pour on the water, the milk (boiling, if it has not been previously pasteurised) and the fruit juice. Stir well to dissolve the sugar. Strain through some nylon net, a sieve or a jelly-bag, then bottle. This punch must be drunk within a few days; if you wish to keep it longer than that before serving do not add the water until the last minute, and then add it boiling, since the punch, of course, should be drunk just warm.

PUNCH

Take two or three good fresh lemons, with rough skins quite yellow; some lumps of good sugar; grate a handful of the skins of the lemons, through a bread grater, on to the sugar; then squeeze in the lemons, bruise the sugar and stir the juice well together, for much depends on the process of mixing the sugar and lemons; pour on them one quart of boiling water, and again mix them well together (this is called the sherbet); add one pint and a half of brandy, and the same quantity of rum; stir it up, then strain it through a sieve; put in one quart of syrup, and one quart of boiling water.

RUBY DELIGHT

And here is a novelty most home winemakers will be able to compile, and which is very popular with the ladies:

½ bottle blackberry wine	Wineglass ginger wine
½ bottle rhubarb wine	Wineglass port wine
½ wineglass whisky	

"WHISKY AND GINGER ALE"

½ oz. essence ginger	1 oz. burnt sugar
½ oz. essence capsicum	2½ lb. brown sugar
¼ oz. Tartaric acid	1 pint white grape concentrate
20 drops essence lemon	9 pints water
5 drops essence vanilla	Yeast and nutrient

Buy the first six ingredients from your chemist, grocer or wine supplies shop.

Put the sugar and grape concentrate in bowl and add boiling water, stir to dissolve both, then stir in tartaric acid and lemon essence. When cool add yeast and nutrient, and ferment in the usual way. When fermentation has finished add the ginger, capsicum and vanilla essences.

Do this by degrees, to taste, since the quantities quoted are the maximum. The final step is to aerate the finished drink in a Sparklets siphon (see p. 38) to produce a beverage very similar to a whisky ginger bought over the bar of an average pub.

INDEX

INDEX

INDEX

INDEX

Other 'AW' Books

Bryan Acton
RECIPES FOR PRIZEWINNING WINES

—recipes for making your own wines are not difficult to come by nowadays: recipes which will produce *quality* wines are. That is where this book can help you. Most of the recipes that it contains have won prizes in national and regional shows, and they have been garnered over several years by Bryan Acton; others have been devised by him to guarantee first-class results. All the recipes in this book, carefully followed, will produce wines of startling quality with the minimum of effort and the maximum of certainty. So if you wish to get among the prizewinners—or even just to produce superb wines for your own satisfaction—this is the book for you!   £1.10, p. & p. 29p

Bryan Acton and Peter Duncan
MAKING WINES LIKE THOSE YOU BUY

—how to make your own Sherry, Port, Madeira, Champagne, Chianti, red and white table and dessert wines, hocks, Moselles, etc. A fascinating chapter tells how to make a whole range of aperitifs (Vermouth, etc.) and liqueurs, and all this at a fraction of what they would cost to buy. The book for the really progressive winemaker. 76 recipes for wines, 56 for liqueurs. Fully illustrated.   £1.00, p. & p. 29p

P. Duncan and B. Acton
PROGRESSIVE WINEMAKING

—this magnificent, fact-packed volume by these two well-known winemaking experts has been hailed as one of the best books of the decade; it deals with advanced winemaking in a readable way, and carries its erudition lightly. This really fat volume—500 pages—is really two books in one. Part I deals with the scientific theory of winemaking, sulphite, acidity, tannin, water, the hydrometer, the meaning of pH, yeast, nutrients, preparation of the must, fermentation, racking, clarification continuous filtering, building a press, blending, fortification, wine disorders, etc. Part II deals with the production of quality wines, both red and white, and the making of Sherry, Port and Madeira type wines, and sparkling wines—all in the greatest detail. Fully illustrated.

Paperback, £1.75, p. & p. 52p
Hardback, £2.50, p. & p. 58p

P. McCall
WINEMAKER'S DICTIONARY

—the most comprehensive and readily available mine of information. Most easily consulted reference book for winemakers, lecturers and shop staffs. £1.20, p. & p. 30p

J. R. Mitchell, L.I.R.C., A.I.F.S.T.
SCIENTIFIC WINEMAKING—MADE EASY

—this is at once the most advanced and most practical textbook on the subject so far, written by a scientist who is a quality control executive employed by a group of companies owning some of Britain's largest wine interests. A glance at the chapter headings shows its scope: The way it should start (sterilisation, etc.); Selecting the right equipment; Extracting and adjusting fruit juices for fermentation; Preparing the yeast starter; Managing the fermentation; Racking, sweetening and fortifying; Aging; Filtration and finings; Bottling; Storing and serving; How to evolve recipes; Tasting and glossary of terms; Micro-organisms of fermentation and spoilage; Troubles and cures; Simplified wine chemistry; and useful test procedures. Packed with new information. Fully illustrated, 260 pages. The book any serious winemaker must have. £1.50, p. & p. 35p

Peter Duncan
WINEMAKING WITH CONCENTRATES

—using American and European concentrates to make delicious wines and using less sugar in the process. 75p, p. & p. 29p

Cedric Austin
WHYS AND WHEREFORES OF WINEMAKING

—this book is outside the usual run of wine manuals. Its primary aim is to produce *better* wine by assisting the winemaker to *understand what he is doing*. For that reason, it is an essential handbook for use at any stage. Here are the pros and cons of different methods set out; the facts and fallacies separated; the function or ingredients and additives explained; the queries and indecisions cleared up. It will help beginners who wonder why recipes vary in ingredient and method to make the same wine, as well as experienced winemakers who, as their skill increases, wish to know why as well as how. The whys and wherefores of winemaking, expressed in a cheerful and readable style, are brought together in six sections, with an index to aid easy reference. 60p, p. & p. 29p

KITZINGER EUROPEAN WINE BOOK

—the famous German yeast culture firm's look at fruit wine making. 50p, p. & p. 23p

Cedric Austin
GOOD WINES OF EUROPE

—this book caters for the ever-increasing public desire to learn or know more about the good wines of Europe. It assumes no previous knowledge, no special ability, only the recognition that drinking wine is one of life's pleasures, and that this pleasure can be increased by knowing what wines to drink.   75p, p. & p. 29p

J. Restall & D. Hebbs
HOW TO MAKE WINES WITH A SPARKLE

—John Restall and Don Hebbs have spent years exploring the techniques of sparkling wine production and in discovering the secrets of producing champagne-like wine of superb quality. This book is the result. If you follow its methods and principles you too can produce impressive sparkling wines which will be the envy and admiration of your winemaking friends.

£1.00, p. & p. 29p

Ren Bellis
EXPRESS WINEMAKING

If you wish to use your own ingredients and make good sound wines, yet have them ready for drinking in a month (or less). This is the book for you.

£1.00, p. & p. 29p

C. J. J. Berry
WINEMAKING WITH CANNED AND DRIED FRUIT

—the simplest, most convenient and most economical of all. How to make delightful wines from the ready-prepared ingredients you can find at your grocers or supermarket, tinned fruits and juices, pulps, purées, pie fillings, concentrates, jams, jellies and dried fruit.   70p, p. & p. 29p

Edited by C. J. J. Berry
"AMATEUR WINEMAKER" RECIPES

—this useful AW paperback contains a fascinatingly varied collection of over 200 recipes garnered from several years' issues of the winemaker's favourite magazine. They include many by that well-known Birmingham winemaker Cyril Shave, a specialist in wines from herbs, and a particularly useful set of recipes for liqueurs, punches, mulls, fruit cups and other party drinks. The cartoons are by Rex Royle.   80p, p. & p. 29p

C. J. J. Berry
130 NEW WINEMAKING RECIPES

—the companion paperback to *First Steps*, augmenting its 150 recipes with 130 others using newly available ingredients. Together these two books give you a unique collection of up-to-date recipes. It is also a complete instruction book in itself. Illustrations, and 50 amusing cartoons by Rex Royle.

£1.00, p. & p. 29p

Dr. F. W. Beech and Dr. A. Pollard
WINEMAKING AND BREWING

—this authoritative new book by these two experts from the Long Ashton Research Station covers the theory and practice of winemaking and brewing in detail; how to grow grapes, how to make wines, perries, ciders, ales, punches, beers, fruit juices and vinegars and how to judge. A really informative paperback.

£1.10, p. & p. 35p

OFF DUTY WINEMAKING

—delightfully simple in text and illustrations. Excellent handbook for the complete beginner. Making wine from concentrate.

£1.20, p. & p. 29p

Bryan Acton and Peter Duncan
MAKING MEAD

—the up-to-date approach to man's most ancient drink. How to make meads (sweet and dry), melomels, hyppocras, metheglin, dyments, cyser, etc., etc. The only full-length paperback on this winemaking speciality available.

£1.00, p. & p. 29p

Dave Line
BREWING BEERS LIKE THOSE YOU BUY

—over 100 recipes to enable you to imitate famous beers from aroung the world. Full instructions for the beginner.

£1.25, p. & p. 29p

C. J. Dart and D. A. Smith
WOODWORK FOR WINEMAKERS

—have your ever wanted to make your own wine press, or fruit pulper, or winery? If you have, then this is the book for you. It explains how over thirty useful pieces of winemaking equipment can be made easily and cheaply at home using only the most elementary tools. The authors give clear and detailed working drawings and instructions in every case.

80p, p. & p. 29p

Tilly Timbrell and Bryan Acton
THE WINEMAKER'S COOKBOOK

—this brilliant book will really make your mouth water! The only one available on this subject, it gives you a whole range of exciting *hors d'oeuvres*, soups, fish, meat, poultry and dessert dishes that can be made using your own home-made wines. *The Winemaker's Cookbook* is essentially practical cookery, demanding no rare and expensive ingredients, all its recipes have been tested and approved by a team of cooks and tasters!

£1.00, p. & p. 23p

Anne Parrack
COMMONSENSE WINEMAKING

—a practical no frills primer in winemaking snd with its aid anyone can quickly and easily be making superb wines.

£1.25, p. & p. 35p

T. Edwin Belt
PLANTS UNSAFE FOR WINEMAKING

—including native or naturalised plants, shrubs and trees which are dangerous, doubtful or dubious as winemaking ingredients, or which can be used only within limitations. 50p, p. & p. 23p

T. Edwin Belt
WILD PLANTS FOR WINEMAKING

—a most detailed guide to all who wish to make their wines from the wild fruits and flowers of the woods and hedgerows, which are there free, for the taking. 80p, p. & p. 23p

T. Edwin Belt
PRESERVING WINEMAKING INGREDIENTS

—a useful AW book, and the only one available dealing with this aspect of winemaking It tells how, in times of plenty or surplus, to preserve fruit, flowers and vegetables for use later in the year, when time and utensils are available. It deals in detail with preservation by means of drying (how to dry, for instance, rose hips, elderberries, sloes, bilberries, apples, etc.), chemical preservation, deep freezing, and chunk bottling. Also how to make syrups, jams and jellies from wild and garden fruit.

60p, p. & p. 29p

Gillian Pearkes
GROWING GRAPES IN BRITAIN

—a handbook for winemakers. Written specially for the English viticulturist, it tells the history of vinegrowing in England, explains that it *is* possible to grow and ripen wine grapes outdoors, and covers fully choice of site and varieties, planting, training, manuring, pruning, pest control, propagation, harvesting and winemaking. The most detailed book available on this subject, and indispensable whether you have six vines or six thousand.

£1.10, p. & p. 29p

N. Poulter
GROWING VINES

—eminently a down-to-earth book. If you wish to produce your own delicate British wines from your own mini-vineyard this book points the way.

60p, p. & p. 20p

N. Poulter
WINES FROM YOUR VINES

—the logical sequence to Mr. Poulter's first book "Growing Vines". Readable and very practical, covering all aspects of winemaking from grapes.

50p, p. & p. 29p

C. J. J. Berry
HOME BREWED BEERS AND STOUTS

—the very first full-length book on this fascinating subject to be published, and still the best; many thousands of copies have been sold. Bang up-to-date, it covers: The story of ale and beer; Types of beer and stout; Background to brewing; Brewing at home from barley, malt, malt extract, dried malt extract, other herbs and grits; How to make lager, pale ale, light, mild, brown, bitter, stout, barley wine, mock beers. We illustrated.

£1.00, p. & p. 29p

C. J. J. Berry
HINTS ON HOME BREWING

—a concise and well-illustrated "rapid course" for home brewers, containing all the basic, down-to-earth essentials.

30p, p. & p. 18p

David Lines
THE BIG BOOK OF BREWING

—acclaimed as THE handbook for the enthusiastic and ambitious amateur brewer, the man who wants to brew really high quality "True" beers. The most advanced and comprehensive book on the subject.   £1.50, p. & p. 35p

T. Edwin Belt
BREW YOUR FAVOURITE PUB BEER

— and avoid the standard mass produced beers that are so often presented—with no alternative.

60p, p. & p. 20p

DURDEN PARK BEER CIRCLE BOOK

—recipes for light ales, pale ales, bitters, brown ales, dry and sweet stouts, lager and barley wine.

50p, p. & p. 17p

Ken Shales
BREWING BETTER BEERS

—a lively paperback on home brewing by a real master of the craft. Ken Shales, of Basildon (which is likely to be renamed Boozledon from now on, it seems!). This book gives Ken's personal, well-tried recipes for all types of malt liquor from lightest lager to blackest double-stout and explains many finer points of brewing technique. A book no really thirsty home brewer should be without!

80p, p. & p. 29p

Ken Shales
ADVANCED HOME BREWING

—the next step from "Brewing Better Beers". This second book is the most advanced one on home brewing available in Great Britain. In it Ken reviews the various ingredients used in brewing and gives his personal recipes for a wide range of popular beers and stouts. Contains much information which is not to be found elsewhere. 70p, p. & p. 29p

Dean Jones
HOME BREWING SIMPLIFIED

—detailed recipes for ten types of bottled and draught beer; hints, tips and know-how. Clear, easy-to-follow directions for successful brewing. 35p, p. & p. 18p

JUDGING HOME-MADE WINES AND BEERS

—the official detailed handbook published by the National Guild of Judges. Essential for all would-be judges and stewards. Full procedure; specimen schedules for all sizes of show; specimen show rules; constitution of Guild; how to qualify as a National Judge. £1.00, p. & p. 17p

PROGRAMME IDEAS

—the AW's printed list to help programme secretaries and others; how to construct a year's Circle programme; where to obtain speakers (on winemaking, brewing, commercial wines and allied subjects) films, coloured slides, social events and ideas, suggestions for outings, wine competitions, lists of judges, etc. 50p, p. & p. 17p

Roy Ekins
WORLDWIDE RECIPES

—an intriguing book of recipes ranging from prickly pears to paw paws to lychees and logans.
75p, p. & p. 24p

For the newcomer as well as the established winemaker......

... we have a full range of ingredients and equipment. Both Boots own brands at superb "value prices" and also most of the leading proprietary makes. We cater for the beginner to the wine makers craft and the advanced enthusiast.

See the complete range at larger Boots branches.

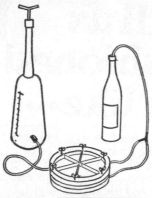

FESTIVAL

THE GRAPE JUICE
CONCENTRATE THAT
ACTUALLY COMES
FROM FRANCE

FESTIVAL (GB) HAVILAND RD., FERNDOWAN IND. EST.
DORSET   Telephone 0202 36644 893722

EDME
SUPERBREW
The complete home brewing kit.
No need to add sugar.

**Superbrew PALE ALE · Superbrew LAGER
Superbrew BITTER · Superbrew STOUT
Superbrew BARLEY WINE**

These 4 lb. kits contain ALL that you need to make first class beer.

Edme have even incorporated the necessary amount of proper brewing sugar with malt and hops for the type of beer to be brewed and concentrated them to a complete kit.

You simply open the can, dissolve the contents in water, add the yeast provided under the cap, and ferment.

Also available are the well-known Edme malt extracts and hopped concentrates for home brewing.

These are:— Edme D.M.S. and Superflavex (S.F.X.) unhopped malt extracts. – Edme ready hopped concentrated worts for Pale Ale, Bitter, Lager, Barley Wine and Stout. Simple instructions on the tin.

THE CHOICE OF THE FIRST CLASS BREWER